Benjamin F Mason

Through War to Peace

Benjamin F Mason

Through War to Peace

ISBN/EAN: 9783744745956

Printed in Europe, USA, Canada, Australia, Japan

Cover: Foto ©ninafisch / pixelio.de

More available books at **www.hansebooks.com**

Benj. F. Mason.

THROUGH
WAR TO PEACE

BY BENJAMIN F. MASON,

Author of the "Village Mystery," or "The Spectres of St. Arlyle."

PUBLISHED FOR THE AUTHOR.

1891.

Entered according to Act of Congress, in the
the year 1891, by

B. F. MASON,

In the Office of the Librarian of Congress, at Washington.

CONTENTS.

CHAPTER I.
THE BATTLE OF BULL RUN, OR MANASSAS.

CHAPTER II.
THE RETREAT FROM THE FIELD OF MANASSAS.

CHAPTER III.
THE SOLDIER'S LAST WATCH.

CHAPTER IV.
THE OLD ENEMY AGAIN.

CHAPTER V.
A NEMESIS ON HIS TRACK.

CHAPTER VI.
JUST IN THE NICK OF TIME.

CHAPTER VII.
THE BATTLE OF CHANCELLORSVILLE.

CHAPTER VIII.
AT REST AT LAST.

CHAPTER IX.
THE BATTLE OF GETTYSBURG.

CHAPTER X.
THE CLOSE OF THE BATTLE OF GETTYSBURG.

CHAPTER XI.
THE STRUGGLE WITH DEATH.

CHAPTER XII.
AT REST IN HEAVEN.

CHAPTER XIII.
NEARING THE END.
CHAPTER XIV.
THE DAWN OF PEACE.
CHAPTER XV.
THE LAST REVIEW OF THE ARMY OF THE POTOMAC.
CHAPTER XVI.
SAD AND SWEET MEMORIES.
CHAPTER XVII.
THE VANDAL CONGRESS ONCE AGAIN.
CHAPTER XVIII.
THE VANDAL CONGRESS CONTINUED.
CHAPTER XIX.
HOME AGAIN IN ST. ARLYLE.
CHAPTER XX.
UNDER THE LIGHT OF PEACE.

Through War To Peace:

A SEQUEL TO
The Village Mystery.

BY BENJAMIN F. MASON.

CHAPTER I.
THE BATTLE OF BULL RUN, OR MANASSA

> HEN shook the hills with thunder riven,
> Then rushed the steeds to battle driven,
> And louder than the bolts of heaven
> Far flashed the red artillery.
> —*Campbell.*

IT was a calm, beautiful Sunday morning, on the 21st of June, 1861; the sun arose in all its splendor and threw its bright rays down on the glens, woods, and clear bubbling streams of the Plain of Manassas; while far away in the distance, robed in their azure hue, stood the tall summits and pinnacles of the Blue Ridge, guarding, like sentinels, around a field of death!

But ere long, ever and anon, the calm was broken by the roar of artillery, and white wreaths of smoke were seen ascending from the cannon's mouth, into the clear, blue sky above the two long, glittering lines of the contending armies, telling of the fearful struggle soon to begin!

It was the battle field of Bull Run, the first great, bloody conflict of the Civil War. Side by side, the men stood in the long, gleaming lines of battle, waiting for the orders to rush forward into the vortex of death! And standing there in that short interval—with thoughts flashing over their minds as thick as waves on an ocean beach—ere they met amid the awful clash of arms, many a soldier's thoughts were wandering far away to Northern and Southern cities and villages, where friends and loved ones were answering the Sabbath bells' sweet peal of love and peace; and many a soldier in his imagination could see dearly loved ones walking up the old familiar church steps, that he knew so well, but that perhaps he would never see again; for before that Sabbath sunlight faded into night many a one would be called to "join that silent number in the land whence none return!"

The St. Arlyle regiment arrived on the field the evening before the battle, and had been assigned to General Hunter's division, one of the first bodies to become engaged on the following morning. There had been during the day several severe but short engagements between the advance skirmishers of the two armies, but they had now fallen back on the main bodies, and all was again quiet. But it was but the lull before the great struggle on the morrow!

It was a beautiful night; the moon was full, and shed a soft, mellow light down from a cloudless sky, while not a breath of wind ruffled the gleaming surface of the rippling streams, or rustled the leaves of the surrounding forest, arrayed in all the brightness of a mid-summer's night, while in every direction thousands of camp-fires glared forth, throwing weird, fantastic shadows against the thick foliage of the trees.

Around one of the numerous camp-fires a party of Vandals were collected, discussing the impending battle.

"Well," said Ned Stanton, "we'll have a lively time to-morrow. Some of us will have to do a good deal of dodging to save our skulls."

"Yah," said Blowhard Jake, "bud by Shimmany! von't ve mak dem Rebil runs!"

"Look out they don't make you run," said another Vandal.

"Not much dey von't!"

"I don't know about that," said Gleaton, "some of you fellows will want to go home mighty bad when the Rebel bullets are whistling around your ears. And then fight the rest of the war with your jaws, in the tailor shop."

"Well," said the Pirate, with his usual nonchalance, "we'll take a few shots at 'em fhirst, ahnyhow, just to kape things loively, afore we lave."

Thus the conversation ran on, for most of them slept but little that night, and eagerly they responded to the rolling of the drums ere daylight broke on Sunday morning. Then followed a rapid march, until they could see the enemy's forces in the distance, when a short halt was ordered. Here we have already described them, waiting for the final order to move on to the attack.

Between the two armies flowed the Bull Run stream, and at a considerable distance from it, on the summit of the ridges, gently sloping to the plain, were posted the Confederate forces, nearly three miles in length. Almost opposite the enemy's center was a stone bridge, spanning the stream, which was guarded by a Confederate regiment.

It was planned by the Federal commander, General McDowell, that a feint attack should be made on the bridge by one of the divisions, while the two others, of Heintzleman and Hunter (the latter containing the St. Arlyle regiment), were to make a detour through the thick woods, and fall upon the enemy's flank and rear.

The battle began a few minutes after six o'clock, by the discharge of a shell from a mortar in the direction of the regiment guarding the stone bridge. Then followed a rapid cannonade from both sides, but the Union forces did not advance to drive the regiment from the bridge, but remained firing at long range, as their desire was to attract the enemy's attention, while the two divisions pushed through the thick forest.

But the Confederates were on the alert, and before long they became aware that a large body of men were pressing through the dense forest toward their left and in their rear. They immediately wheeled around and formed a new and stronger line—as it was on elevated ground, and partly sheltered by the houses, barns, sheds, haystacks and fences of a farm situated there—and at the same time rapidly reinforcing the line to meet the attack of the Federals.

Meanwhile, the divisions having forded the Bull Run stream, and filled their canteens with water, were pressing on as rapidly through the woods as the tangled vines and thick undergrowth would permit. But their progress was so retarded that it was ten o'clock before the advance brigade reached the open field.

Among the first troops to reach the edge of the wood was Landon's regiment, and as they came into the open ground they were received with a perfect storm of cannon balls and bullets from the enemy's elevated position. The severe fire for a few moments made the raw troops recoil, as the dead and wounded fell around them, but they were pressed forward by those in the rear, and were soon rushing up the rising ground, sharply replying to the enemy's fire, while several batteries of artillery had emerged from the wood and were firing over their heads with telling effect on the Confederates.

" Bejabers!" exclaimed Kelly, wildly, "it's extramely loively! An' thar aint mouch fun fightin' Ribils!"

"No," replied his comrade, also a Vandal, "I'd rather be back in the tailor shop."

" Dunder und blitzen!" yelled Jake, "dey mights hit somebodies in der eye!"

"Put yer eyes in yer phocket!" answered the Pirate.

"Shiver me timbers!" cried Sailor Jack, as he glanced down the line, "ef the boys aint fallin' overboard lively!"

They were now in the hottest part of the battle, and there was no longer any time for words, as they pressed rapidly up the hillside, firing volley after volley at the Confederate ranks, while bullets and balls went plowing through their own. Each moment fresh companies of troops emerged from the wood and rushed up the gentle slope, till the Confederate commander, Evans, was on the point of falling back, when he was reinforced by Gen. Bee's division. The National forces were now sorely pressed, but they were rapidly supported and their line greatly strengthened. The battle now raged desperately, the air was filled with bullets, cannon balls and shells; the dead and wounded lay thick on the field, while the roar of the firearms was almost deafening. Although the enemy, from his elevated position, was doing terrible execution—especially with his artillery—on the National line, the rapid reinforcement of the latter was slowly pressing his lines back. Just at this time the Federals were again reinforced by Sherman's brigade, and the Confederates could resist no longer and began a retreat. Over the ridge and down the southern slope of a small valley the Confederates fled, but in good order, as they were aided in the retreat by Hampton's famous legion, which had just arrived on the field. Across the valley they rushed, and up a gentle slope leading to a large plateau above, closely followed by their pursuers.

Cheers broke from the Federal lines, as they considered the victory complete, and the commanders were already congratulating each other, when suddenly an incident of determination and valor occurred, that turned the tide of victory.

As the flying troops, under General Bee, reached the brow of the plateau there stood a brigade drawn up in line of battle, seemingly as immovable as the rocks themselves, waiting for the coming struggle. At its head sat a commander whose name became famous on many a bloody field in after years. It was Gen. T. J. Jackson.

General Bee rode up to the tall Virginian, who sat on his horse with a face like marble, and exclaimed, with despair imprinted on every line of his face: "General, they are beating us back!"

"Then, sir," answered Jackson, calmly, "we'll give them the bayonet!"

The words sent a thrill of hope through the disheartened Bee, and turning to his men, he exclaimed: "There are Jackson and his Virginians standing like a *stone wall!*"

And ever after he was known as Stonewall Jackson.

Although the Confederates had been driven up the hill to the plateau above, Jackson's stubborn resistance here held the Federals in check, while the former were rapidly reinforced with infantry and artillery, and took up a strong position on the brow, sheltered by the thicket of pines. Up these hillsides, against this strong line, the Federals hurled brigade after brigade, till the slopes were black with men. It was now afternoon, and the heat was intense. The battle raged fiercely, the roar of the conflict was terrific, as the cannons belched forth their thunder, mingled with the crash of the musketry, the heavy tramp of the cavalry, the screams and groans of the wounded, and the shrill shriek of the bursting shell. The air was thick with dust and smoke, completely hiding the combatants from each other, as if struggling in a mist, while red flashes of flame darted high into the air above the pandemonium of death and destruction. The Confederates were inferior in numbers to the attacking forces, but they had by far the advantage, in their elevated position, and the cover afforded by the pine trees. And from the elevation the Confederates poured a raking artillery fire into the advancing masses. But on the National soldiers came, every moment pressing the enemy harder. At last the critical moment had arrived. The loss had been severe on both sides. Though the Federals had not broken the enemy's line, the latter's situation had now become desperate. Every one of their available men had long since been hurried to the heart of the struggle, while on the National side fresh troops were already hurrying to the front. The Confederate generals Bee and Baxter had been killed, Jackson and Hampton wounded.

"Oh, for a brigade!" cried the Confederate commander to a staff officer.

At this period, to add to General Beauregard's despair, telegraphic signals warned him to look out for a body of troops advancing on his left.

"At this moment," said Gen. Beauregard in mentioning the occurrence afterward, " I must confess my heart failed me."

It was a strong column of men, and at their head was a flag, but Beauregard could not tell, even through a strong field glass, whether it was the stars and bars or the stars and stripes.

A look of despair and sadness swept over the Confederate General's face, as he turned to an officer and ordered him to hasten to General Johnston and request him do what he could to support and protect a retreat.

Again Gen. Beauregard fixed one last lingering gaze through his field-glass upon the advancing flag, but he could not distinguish it, as it hung limply around the staff. But, just as he was lowering his spy-glass, a gentle breeze sprang up, and slowly, steadily, the banner unfolded and floated full out on the warm air. It was the stars and *bars!* Instantly the Confederate General's face lighted up with triumph and pleasure, as he cried exultantly to a staff officer:

"Col. Evans, ride forward and order Gen. Kirby Smith to hurry up his command, and strike them on the flank and rear!"

The advancing troops, under Kirby Smith, were a part of Johnston's army from the Shenandoah Valley, that had eluded the Federal General, Patterson, who was to have held them in check. They were moving toward Manassas Junction by railway, when Kirby Smith, hearing the heavy firing, knew that a great battle was in progress. So he stopped the engine before reaching the Junction, and, forming his men, pushed forward to the struggle.

The fresh command struck the National troops full on the right flank, ere they could form a new line. For a few moments the Union right fought desperately, but their efforts were in vain. Flanked and under a terrible cross fire, they were forced to fall back, slowly at first, then more rapidly. As the Federals saw their right wing fall back in confusion, the cry rapidly went along the line:

" Here's Johnston from the Valley! Here's Johnston from the Valley!" And in a few minutes the entire army began to retreat, and then broke into a wild rout. The battle was lost.

CHAPTER II.

THE RETREAT FROM THE BATTLE FIELD OF MANASSAS.

> FOR those that fly may fight again,
> Which he can never do that's slain;
> Hence timely running's no mean part
> Of conduct in the martial art.
> —*Butler.*

AMONG the few regiments that retained their order, and remained firm to the last, was the St. Arlyle one. But at last, far outnumbered by the enemy, and each moment being cut through by their own fugitive infantry and artillery, they were forced to scatter in every direction. Gleaton's company formed a part of the extreme left of the regiment, and, unlike the rest of the command, was unprotected by the bushes and undergrowth; therefore was the first to be overrun by the flying artillery and cavalry. Helter skelter his men fled to escape the wheels of the cannons and the hoofs of the horses. Gleaton soon found himself, to use his own expression, "in command of himself only." He ran on for quite a distance, till he came to a clump of bushes—where another Vandal had already taken refuge—when he sprang behind them. But ere long the enemy's bullets began to whistle thick around their heads, and it got by far too hot to be comfortable, as Gleaton remarked to his companion, laughingly:

> "'As custom arbitrates, whose shifting sway
> Our lives and manners must alike obey.'
> So I guess we'd better run away."

But Gleaton was a little too late in this movement, for before he could reach the open ground he was captured by two Confederates, who, seizing him by each arm, led him rapidly through the thicket toward their lines. But as they were emerging from the undergrowth with their prisoner they were suddenly met by a flying piece of artillery, which knocked one of the Confederates down, while the other and Gleaton had just time to spring out of its way. Finding himself free, Gleaton sprang quickly forward, just as the muzzle of the gun was passing, and, seizing hold of it, with a strong effort swung himself up on the breech, where he clung desperately, as he yelled at the discomfited Confederate:

"'Fare thee well! yet think awhile
On one whose bosom bleeds to doubt thee!'"

The soldier also proved to be a wit, for he replied, in the words of Pope:

"I hold sage Homer's rule the best,
Welcome the coming, speed the going guest!"

And, by way of emphasizing his words, he fired point blank at Gleaton, but, luckily for the ex-blacksmith, the ball went wide of its mark.

Let us now turn to Marshall. When his men scattered and left him alone, he started to run rapidly toward the rear, when he was halted by the enemy, who had nearly surrounded him.

"Surrender!" shouted one of the Confederates, "you're our prisoner!"

"Ah! yes, indeed; I've been looking for some one to surrender to," he exclaimed, as he threw up his arms.

But at the same time, seeing an opening in the underbrush, he popped into it, as he remarked in his usual reckless manner:

"The mouse that always trusts to one poor hole
Can never be a mouse of any soul!"

But he did not escape without a volley of harmless bullets following him. At least they were harmless so far as he was concerned, for none of them struck him. He ran through the thicket, and near its edge finding a disabled baggage wagon, he cut a mule loose from the traces, and mounting him, started "to leave the field," as he afterward said, "as a cavalryman," but, the mule not going fast enough, he struck him, when the animal suddenly stopped, and, rearing up behind, the ex-editor shot over his head, or, as Marshall afterward told it in rhyme:

"I seized and mounted a black artillery mule,
Made up my mind that he or I must rule;
But as I raised the whip o'er his left ear,
The mule raised up his heels and shed a muleteer!"

The rest of the way the ex-editor pursued on foot. For, as he remarked, he didn't wish to ride mules, as he "didn't understand their nature." Besides, he didn't like the "feeling" way the animal had of "shedding a muleteer!" "It sort of annihilated, kind of Vandalized a fellow."

Another Vandal, who was tardy in "beating" a retreat, was Sailor Jack. And, being far behind the rest, he became confused, and ran in the wrong direction—toward the enemy's lines. As he subsequently expressed it, "he got befogged and went sailing around on a dead reckoning."

At last he became surrounded by the Confederates in nearly every direction, and the bullets whistling around his head as thick as hail on a winter's day.

"Shiver me timbers!" he exclaimed, "ef there's much chance to go fore or aft. So I guess I'll take a starboard tack," he continued, as he fled into a neighboring wood.

Of all the Vandals, only one was severely wounded. That was Jim Kelly, though several others received slight bruises, though not bad enough to necessitate their entering the hospital. But poor Kelly had received a dangerous gash in the side, and had just strength enough left to crawl behind a tree, before he swooned away from the loss of blood. Here he was found the next day, and carried to the hospital by a number of Vandals, who had gone out in search of him.

"Be jabers, boys," said he, between his groans of pain, as they raised him on the stretcher, "they kum mighty near sinkin' this pirate. They put an awful big howl in 'er side."

Of the remaining Vandals, Frank Meredith and Dave Johnson were taken prisoners, or, as Gleaton remarked, "the Rebels borrowed them fer awhile."

But there was one Vandal the "Rebels" did not "borrow" or shoot. True, he did not give them much of a chance to do either—that was Blowhard Jake. Almost at the first fire his courage "oozed out," so to speak, and he took French leave. As he was starting toward the rear one of the officers ordered him back, but this only accelerated his motion.

"Never mind him," remarked Marshall, "he's only going off to catch his breath."

But it took Jake a long while to "catch his breath," for he did not stop retreating until he got back to St. Arlyle, and he never returned, for he had enough of war for the rest of his life.

"Dunder und blitzen!" he used to exclaim, in speaking of the battle afterward, "dem Rebils mights er hit er feller in der eye!"

He seemed to have a great respect for his eyes.

As Marshall ran onward, after being so unceremoniously dismounted from the mule, he overtook Gleaton, who was also journeying along on foot, having tumbled off his seat on the cannon.

"Hello, *Captain* Marshall!" exclaimed the latter, emphasizing the word "Captain," "why don't you rally your men, and make a brave stand and turn the tide of battle?"

"Ah," replied the ex-editor,

"My tongue within my lips I rein,
For who talks much must talk in vain."

"But why don't *you, Captain* Gleaton?"

"I have given a very good command, and I think they'll obey it. It's found in Shakespeare, and it is: 'Sweep on, you fat and greasy citizens.' But what do you think of things in general, Marshall?"

"They seem to be mixed; in fact, sort of annihilated, kind of Vandalized."

At this moment they came upon a mounted officer, who was making a buncombe speech to the flying men, urging them to rally and drive back the enemy. But all the while the officer's horse's head was turned toward the rear, and the warrior himself was every few seconds casting furtive glances toward the enemy, so as to be ready to flee at a moment's notice of danger.

"Fine words; I wonder where he stole 'em," exclaimed Gleaton, just as the officer rode away at full speed toward the rear as he caught sight of Stewart's Confederate cavalry in the far distance.

"That fellow," said Marshall, as he watched him disappear, "has mistaken his calling. He was made for an orator, not a warrior."

The rout had now turned into a panic. All kinds of encumbrances had been thrown away. The field was strewn with muskets, belts, knapsacks and every conceivable kind of baggage and article, while the huge, surging mass, without form or order, rushed on to Centerville, and from there to Washington. In this huge, chaotic crowd, mingling with the soldiers, were citizens, members of Congress, governors and various other State officials and their wives, who were now all fleeing for dear life, some in carriages, others on foot, leaving behind them elegant lunches and forgotten speeches, which they had intended to make over a glorious victory.

As Gleaton and Marshall hurried onward they passed a group of soldiers surrounding a large table cloth, on which was spread some flown Congressman's banquet, of savory dishes and bottles of wine. They would hardly have noticed the cluster of men had they not heard their names called. Looking toward the impromptu banqueters, they saw two Vandals seated in their midst, helping themselves to the wine and other good things, perfectly regardless of the enemy's bullets.

"Come on, Marshall! Come, Gleaton!" they shouted. "There's a mighty good spread-out here! The best you ever saw in your life!"

"Look out," answered Gleaton, "the Rebels don't borrow you."

"Oh, confound the Rebels! this is a Vandal lay-out!"

But they were shortly afterward interrupted in their revelry by their Colonel, Charlie Landon, who compelled them to move onward. During the battle Charlie had set his men a brave example, for he had rushed to every part of his line, regardless of the enemy's fire, whenever he saw the men heavily pressed, and encouraged them with words and deeds. And when the retreat began he actively engaged himself in trying to save any of his men from being captured, for he was among the last to leave the field.

"Move on, boys!" he cried. "Don't let the enemy capture you, for we'll want you all another day. I know the battle is lost, and there is no alternative but to retreat. But we'll whip them the next time, and we want every one of you to help. Fight your way through their ranks. Don't let them take you prisoners!"

Charles Landon had generously given his horse to one of his wounded men to ride, and had filled, with the aid of others, an ambulance with the wounded of the regiment, when a mob of wild, excited men sprang forward to jump into the wagon upon the wounded. Instantly Charlie sprang in front of them and drew his sword.

"Back!" he cried. "Shame on you, to attempt to impose on wounded men!"

But the excited crowd still pressed forward. Then the brave firmness of his nature showed itself—the ring of the true metal in the man, as he exclaimed:

"The first man who attempts to spring into that ambulance, I'll run my sword through him!"

The mass halted, for the calm determination of that pale, handsome face awed them even if it did not win their admiration, and then they slowly fell back, and the wagon proceeded unmolested.

Thus ended disastrously to the National cause the first important battle of the War. On both sides there had been some skillful movements, and never, perhaps, in the world's history had raw men done such good fighting. Had the Confederates pushed forward they might easily have captured Washington City. But they were evidently afraid of risking a defeat, for they had not forgotten that they had been beaten back in the early part of the battle, and they were not sure it might not occur again. They were not aware of the fact that when an army is completely routed it falls an easy prey to the victors; besides, they had not yet been hardened to blood and death. For there is no thorough school of the soldier, except by months of experience on the field of strife—an experience they gained long before the close of the War. But so also had their opponents.

After this battle came a quiet, but it was but the lull before the storm of the most bloody and destructive war the American continent had ever yet known. And during its progress the production of as fine soldiers and martial equipments as the world had ever seen. In the meantime each side began raising and organizing immense armies of men. President Lincoln's first call, after the battle, was for a half a million of men. Gen. McDowell was removed from the command of the army around Washington, and superseded by Gen. McClellan.

Then followed the difficult task of organizing and drilling the demoralized mass. General McClellan proved equal to the exigency, and in a few months had succeeded in converting these raw men into a finely disciplined army, well prepared for the bloody work in store for it.

CHAPTER III.

THE SOLDIER'S LAST WATCH.

"OH! once was felt the storm of war!
    It had an earthquake's roar;
It flashed upon the mountain's height,
And smoked along the shore.
It thundered in the dreaming ear,
And up the farmer sprang;
It muttered in a bold, true heart,
And a warrior's harness rang."

NEARLY a year had flown on the wings of Time since the Battle of Manassas. Bertha had been a nurse in the Army of the Potomac nearly seven months. General McClellan had made his famous Peninsula campaign—those seven days of continual fighting—a series of the most desperate and bloody battles that had ever yet been fought on the American continent, beginning with the field at Oak Grove, then followed each successive day, by the terrible contests of Mechanicsville, Gain's Mill, Savage Station, White Oak Swamp, Glendale and the final fierce and bloody struggle at Malvern Hill, and now the army had fallen back and was lying on the James River.

This campaign, one of the most memorable in history, on account of its severe and protracted fighting, had cost the Federal army, in sick, wounded and killed, thousands upon thousands of men. The multitude of hospitals hastily improvised in barns, churches, tents and every variety of building, were filled to overflowing, and Bertha and the many other noble women found plenty of work for their willing hands to do.

These months of service among the wounded were fast winning for Bertha in the Army of the Potomac a fame almost rivaling that of Florence Nightingale in the Crimea. For the busy months of work had made her an efficient nurse, by teaching her to bravely control her nerves and remain calm while assisting to dress those frightful wounds which soldiers receive in warfare, and also how to make and administer the sedative and cooling potions to the fever-parched lips. Once, only, in her trying service did she faint. It was while engaged in bandaging a severe wound in an officer's arm. The ligature of the artery broke, and the hot blood spurted in a flood over her white dress. Her head grew dizzy, while her heart seemed to cease beating, and she would have fallen had not a surgeon caught her and placed her on the bed. When she recovered, which she rapidly did, she found that the surgeon had ligated the artery again, and was bathing her face.

"These are terrible sights, my little lady," said the surgeon, kindly, when she had opened her eyes again. "I am afraid they will prove too much for you."

"Oh no!" she replied, "I shall try and be stronger the next time."

After that when serious accidents occurred (for they often did) she pressed her thumb upon the artery, thus stopping the flow of blood, and quietly awaited the arrival of the surgeon. Thus when she found she could be truly useful to the wounded, she threw herself with her whole heart into the noble work. And many were the blessings showered upon the handsome little lady's head by the suffering men, as she knelt by their beds and administered to their wants, ever with words of kindness. For a soldier in pain can fully appreciate the soft, magic touch of a woman's hand.

Rough and bad as some of these men had been, they never forgot her noble kindness, and when many of them were again able to leave the hospital, they could not employ words enough in which to praise her to others. And afterwards, when she passed groups of soldiers, containing, perhaps, but a single one who had ever known her gentle care (but he had informed the rest) every cap was raised, their boisterous laughter ceased, and a silence fell upon them, as if they were in the presence of an angel.

It is no idle fancy that wins this respect from men. For a noble woman is God's sublimest work on earth. The brightest and richest diadem beneath the blue of heaven. Her example good men love to follow, and even evil ones learn to admire. Noble, kind and true, she leaves a record through the flood of years that time can never efface. She has planted and nourished the blossoms that will bloom beyond the skies. For there is a power in a good woman's magic touch naught else can win. It is the one foretaste of heaven that few but a wounded soldier has ever learned to feel, as she kneels by his side amid the conflict, and does a noble work of mercy.

Bertha, during all these months in the army, had had but several conversations with Charlie Landon, for, although when they met it was in a very friendly way, there was a constraint in their manners that touched a tender chord in their hearts—and actually made the interview painful—as it became impressed upon their minds that they were drifting farther and farther apart.

But oh, how he longed at each meeting to place his arm about her and tell her of the never-ceasing love beating in his heart, as he called himself a thousand times a brute for his treatment of her affections! "But alas!" he thought, "I have crushed the last spark of fondness from her heart by my contemptible actions! And I will not try to degrade or annoy her by offering a love that must be distasteful."

So that powerful control of his nature crushed down every impulse of his heart, and he met her as calmly as if she were but a mere chance acquaintance.

And at these moments in her bosom what a wealth of tenderness lingered for the man she loved, no words could express. But these many days of experience with danger, death and care had taught her well the lesson of self control. So when chance threw them together her little hand touched his without a quiver, while the beautiful, pale face showed not a sign of the strong emotions that were struggling in the little heart.

Of course Bertha found life in the army fraught with many hardships and trials, but there was a consolation for all its inconveniences, in being surrounded by so many friends of her youth. Though she met Charlie but seldom, she saw him often, and that was a pleasure that always had a lingering, inexpressible sweetness about it. Then, too, her true, noble friend, Dr. Granville, was nearly always near, ever ready to assist and encourage her. And then there were the other young men from St. Arlyle, not that she had known them much in former years, but they were from her native village, around which sweet memories still clung. And then, too, in the past year, they had been so linked in her fortunes and misfortunes, that almost unconsciously a strong friendship had grown up between the little lady and them For it is said, and truly, indeed, that kindred works, or trials, make kindred friendships too. And they, on their part, were always ready to add to her comfort or pleasure by bringing her flowers, fruits or other gifts, often fraught with great difficulty to obtain, in that war-swept country. Thus, surrounded by so many well-wishers, gradually came a home-like feeling in her heart. For there is nothing that constitutes home so truly as to be near friends and those dear ones we love the best.

It was the evening of the 7th of July, but a week after the last battle at Malvern Hill; the Army of the Potomac was still encamped on the James River, and in the homes in every part of the Republic were still fresh the memories of the dead, as mothers, wives, sisters and sweethearts were sadly treasuring up the last mementoes of the loved ones, sleeping forever in unmarked soldiers' graves in old Virginia!

The night set in bright and clear, but ere long a fog began drifting in from the bay, each hour growing denser, till it enveloped the two armies like a mantle, and hid from the Federal forces their long picket line, nearly two miles distant.

At the extremity of the line, where it touched the river, James Kelly was standing guard in the silent gloom—silent and gloomy indeed, except for the occasional report and flash of a musket from his own line or that of the enemy, for the outposts of the contending armies were so near together that they could hear the challenges of each others' officers as they went their rounds.

It was just 8 o'clock when Kelly took his place on duty, relieving the former sentinel. The mist had already begun to rapidly envelope the field, and as he stood at his post and watched wistfully, almost sadly, the last gleam of the distant camp fires fade away in the gathering gloom—shutting him in on his lonely vigil—there came a presentiment over the young soldier's heart that the old life had faded too. For an indescribable something seemed to tell him that it was his last watch on earth. But in spite of his fears not a thought of deserting his post of duty ever crossed the brave young fellow's breast.

At 10 o'clock the relief came, but he gave no answer to the challenge, so another sentinel was placed on his post. Again, at midnight, the guard was changed, but there were no signs of the young soldier. He was hidden from view in the mist. Once more the night wore on. At last, when daylight broke, and the warm beams of the sun had melted away the mist, they found the brave young fellow lying at his post! A deep, crimson stain on the rough blue coat, just above his heart, told the sad story that he was "off duty" forever! His eyes were gently closed, as if in sleep, while on the cold lips was even impressed a smile, telling that his death had been sudden and painless. The pale face was wet with dew, as if, for fullfilling his duty, Heaven had thrown down its cold kiss of approval there!

His comrades raised his body gently, and as they bore it away their weather-roughened faces softened and their eyes grew moist. Even the enemy's pickets, who were separated from them by but a narrow cornfield, dropped the butts of their muskets on the ground and waited in respectful silence till the dead soldier was borne from the field. Such was often the kindness shown on both sides for the dead and wounded. Is it any wonder, then, that the war was scarcely over before these same men who had crossed arms in deadly conflict began to bridge over the bloody chasm, by forgiving and forgetting, till it seemed that the Republic was growing stronger in the union of hearts than ever?

Just before sunset that day all that was mortal of James Kelly was brought in a rough pine coffin to its last resting place—a grave dug under a willow, near the river. Bertha had twined a wreath of white roses and geraniums—which she had gathered at a neighboring farm house—and placed it on his breast, as a tribute of her friendship. Around the coffin were gathered the men from St. Arlyle—the friends of bygone years. They removed the lid, and as each was taking a last lingering look, Bertha knelt down and severed a lock of his brown hair and pressed the cold lips that could never more know or feel a kiss - unless spirits can come back again from that land beyond the skies.

Bertha arose, and as the tears stole down her cheeks, said:

"Poor fellow! he's had a rugged life! But he's at last at rest! Let us hope on heaven's bright shore! He once did me a noble favor, and I shall always retain a warm place in my heart for his memory!"

"Yes,' said Charlie Landon, "he was as much a hero as the greatest general in the army, for he gave all he could give for his country—his life!"

The chaplain then read the short burial service, and when it was ended the escort fired three volleys over the grave and quickly strong arms hid him from mortal view. And the friends of bygone years turned sorrowfully back to camp, as they felt that a link was missing in the silver chain of friendship; endeared by the association of years, till it almost twined with the golden chain of love!

CHAPTER IV.

THE OLD ENEMY AGAIN.

<blockquote>
An open foe may be a curse,
But a pretended friend is worse.
—Gay.
</blockquote>

LATE one afternoon, a few days after the great Battle of Antietam, while Bertha was busily engaged in attending the wounded in one of the large hospital tents, where they had been crowded, a letter was handed to her. After dressing the soldier's arm she was attending, she took the letter and examined the directions. They were written in bold, round letters, and addressed to "Miss Bertha Merton." Hastily taking the note out of the envelope, for it was not sealed, she read as follows:

"MISS MERTON: A very dear friend is lying dangerously wounded, perhaps dying. Will you come?" * * *

Then followed a description by which she could find the place. It was a small cottage situated nearly three miles away, and fully a mile beyond the Federal outposts, and nearly six miles from one of the enemy's main bodies, which lay encamped across the Potomac River.

As she read the epistle her heart gave a wild throb of fear and pain, and it was all she could do to choke back the tears as she thought: "Is it dear, kind May who is wounded and dying? Oh, what a cruel thing is war! It has not even spared dear, innocent May!" And then, in spite of all her control, she burst into tears.

"Yes, I will go to her instantly." So, seizing her hat and cloak, she started to leave the hospital, when suddenly she remembered that she had an engagement with Marshall to visit one of the young men from St. Arlyle, who was lying wounded in another tent. So she sealed the letter, and, handing it to a surgeon, requested him to give it to Major Marshall when he called, saying that it would explain itself. Also requesting the doctor to tell Marshall that she would immediately visit the sick soldier on her return, she hastened away.

When she started the last beams of day were fast fading, and ere she reached the outposts of the army it was quite dark. But she kept on in the right direction, for she was too well acquainted with the neighboring country to lose her way. When she reached the Federal pickets there was a soldier on guard whom she knew, and he allowed her to pass without any questions. Leaving the Union lines, she walked rapidly, yet cautiously, toward the enemy. When within a couple of hundred yards of the cottage, she suddenly came upon an advanced post of Confederates—evidently a reconnoitering party which had crossed the river—consisting of three men, one of whom cried:

"Halt! Who goes there?"

But before she could reply one of his comrades said:

"It's a lady. One of the officer's wives, I guess. Let her pass."

Years after, when the war was over, she learned that the soldier who had spoken last was a Vandal who had left St. Arlyle and joined the Confederate army. He had instantly recognized her, and had made up his mind that she should pass unmolested.

The direction in the letter had been so plain that she easily found the house. Crossing the small garden in front of it, she stood knocking at the door before a thought of fear or of her strange situation crossed her mind. For her brain was so excited by emotion that, though her long walk had almost exhausted her strength, she was scarcely aware of it.

On knocking at the door a muffled voice within cried: "Come in."

Pushing open the door, she entered. The apartment was almost in darkness, except for a lamp burning dimly. Her first thoughts were of May, as she walked to a bed in one corner and drew back the covering. It was unoccupied. At that instant the lamp was turned up, flooding the room with light, and the next moment a hand was laid on her shoulder. She started, and, looking up, saw the face of *John Shackle!*

Her heart gave a wild bound of terror, and her pale face grew even whiter as she felt she was again in this villain's power!

"Well, we've met again!" he said, triumphantly, while a sardonic grin curled his flabby lips.

"So I see," she said, calmly, rapidly regaining her self-possession.

"You take it very coolly," he exclaimed, sarcastically.

But he immediately recognized that she was no longer the innocent though clever girl of a few months before; but a woman, whom experience with the world had rendered wiser and more discerning, though it had robbed her of none of the noble sweetness of her nature.

"What else could I do?" she asked, demurely.

"You are not as innocent as you pretend to be," he replied, mockingly.

"Perhaps not; but, as I said before, what am I to do? Cry?"

"No," he said, sharply, "it wouldn't do you any good if you did."

"No, of course not. But why cannot we be friends?"

"Are you sincere?"

"Why should I not be? You have never injured me."

"No, not that I remember. But are you willing to aid me?"

"Yes, if your requests are reasonable."

"But who is to be the judge of that? You or I?"

"Both of us, I suppose," she replied, smiling.

"Yes, it takes two to make a bargain."

"Then state your proposition."

"Not quite yet, my lady. You think you're sharp, don't you? But I'm a lawyer, and I know what's what."

"No, I don't think I'm a match for you."

"Oh, you don't!" sarcastically.

"No indeed, Mr. Shackle."

"I supposed you did," he said, sneeringly.

"But I do not."

"You escaped from me nicely last time. I suppose you think you can do it again?"

"I don't see much of a chance," she said, laughing.

"Neither do I. I've got you in my power this time."

"Yes, I suppose so," she replied, looking furtively toward the door.

He saw her glances, as he said, triumphantly: "You needn t look at the door. I've locked it. Now why don't you cry?"

"Why should I? You are not my enemy. You never did me an injury."

"Then why did you run away before?"

"Because I was younger then, and knew no better."

"I suppose you are smarter now," he said, sneeringly.

"I don't know."

"You wouldn't run away now, because you haven't the chance."

"No," she answered, laughing.

"No, of course not," he said, as involuntarily a smile crossed his lips. "You don't do anything you can't."

"No, never," smiling.

"I suppose you thought the English detectives had me safe long ago. But I was too sharp for them."

"Yes, I see you were."

A look of pride swept over his face at her answer, as he said:

"Yes, those London detectives will find me a match for them. I've thrown them entirely off the scent this time. They do not even dream that I am in the Confederate States. They were looking for me in Canada, the last time I heard from them. They imagine themselves very smart, but I'll show them a trick worth two of theirs! I'll allure them here. And then, you know, in a war-swept country like this, it is not an unusual thing to see a man with a bullet hole through his head, or a bayonet thrust in his heart! It doesn't even excite comment. I'll soon have them out of the way, when I once get them here. It's annoying, to say the least, to have these London devils dogging one around. But I'll give them more than they bargained for! But there is one thing I need to accomplish my little scheme—that is money. And you can help me obtain it. You must!"

"Yes," she replied, "but as you are, perhaps, well aware, I have none with me. But I can return to the Federal camp and undoubtedly obtain it for you," she continued, eagerly, as her heart beat exultingly at the thought of escape.

"No doubt you could, if you would do so. But if you were once to get back to the Federal lines you would forget all about me. Your dear little memory would be very short."

"No, I will surely fulfill my promise if you will let me go."

"I doubt it."

"I will swear to it!" she cried, desperately.

"I have no doubt. But I don't mean to trust you. I don't intend to be hoodwinked."

"But I will surely fulfill my promise," she cried, earnestly.

"Words are cheap, my lady. But you are dealing with too sharp a man to so easily escape. So don't waste your breath."

"Then how can I obtain you the money?"

"Easily enough. Sign this check on the bank in the city near St. Arlyle, and I can soon obtain the money."

"I am not aware that I have a cent in that bank."

"I will take my chances on that."

"I don't think the bank authorities are familiar with my signature. For if I have any money there my father deposited it."

"I will attend to that. *Sign* this check."

"But," she said, "if you will let me go back I will certainly obtain the money for you if it lies in my power. I swear it!"

"I see what is in your mind. It is escape. But it is no use! You are only wasting words. *Sign* this check. For I inform you, *most emphatically*, that all your promises and protests are wasted on me."

"But if you would——"

"*Confound it!*" he interrupted, angrily, "you are only wasting words, and making a fool of yourself! *Sign!* I tell you, *sign!*"

"But will you let me return, if I sign it?"

"*Yes,*" he said, gruffly.

"Upon your honor?"

"Of course I will, *you little fool!*" he exclaimed, angrily. "*What in thunder* do you suppose I would want *with you?*"

"Very well," she answered, as she seated herself at the little stand.

"Now," he said, "don't try to disguise your handwriting, or I'll make you write it over again."

"No, I will not," she said, as she read the paper over. Then, adding her name to it, she arose, saying:

"Now, will you let me go?"

"No, I'm not through with you yet. Do you suppose I am such an idiot as to allow you to go and have the payment of the check stopped?"

"But I will swear to heaven that I will not do so," she exclaimed, excitedly.

"Bah! no more of your promises. Have I not told you often enough I would not trust you? You are only wasting your breath!"

"But you promised to release me."

"Well, what of it?"

"Then you told a falsehood."

"That don't trouble my conscience much. I've told many a lie before."

"But what am I to do? I can't stay here," she cried, pathetically.

"No, of course not. I will take you with me to the Confederate camp. How do you like the proposition?"

"I don't like it," she said, tremblingly.

"I supposed you wouldn't."

"Are you an officer of the Confederate army?" she asked, suddenly.

"No."

"Then—" she commenced, but suddenly stopped.

"Then," he said, divining her question, "what am I doing in it? I pretend to be a war correspondent, but that is a mere blind, while I work out a scheme of mine. My name is now Charles Thorne. And don't you forget it. So you don't like the proposition?"

"No," she said, struggling hard to keep back her temper, fearing his violence.

"Well, there is a way to avoid it. You have requested that we might be friends."

"Yes," shortly.

"And I have nothing against you, although your stubbornness came near getting me into a serious difficulty once. But I will let that pass. Of course you are aware that you are deucedly pretty, in spite of all your mulishness?"

Instinctively she divined his meaning, but fear and anger kept her silent.

"Well, I won't be hard on you," he continued, after waiting several moments for her to speak. "Now, if you will accept my proposition, you may go back to the Federal camp. It is that you will swear before heaven that you will marry me within a year."

"NEVER!" she cried, the whole indignation and scorn of her nature flashing forth in her face and large, black eyes.

"Then I'll RUIN YOU!!" he yelled, as a demoniacal expression of anger swept over his distorted face, that sent a thrill of terror through her heart.

CHAPTER V.

A NEMESIS ON HIS TRACK.

> TIME at last sets all things even;
> And if we do but watch the hour,
> There never yet was human power,
> Which could evade, if unforgiven,
> The patient search, and vigil long,
> Of him who treasures up a wrong.
> —*Byron.*

ABOUT half an hour after Bertha left the hospital tent, Marshall entered and inquired for her. He soon found the surgeon to whom she had given the letter, and as he gave it to Marshall he remarked that Miss Merton had said that it would explain all. On receiving the epistle, Marshall walked to an opening in the tent, and hastily glanced at the address in the fast waning daylight. He knew the handwriting in an instant. And over his face came an expression of anger and determination, that rapidly became mingled with sadness, as the writing recalled the bitter memories of long fled years. He tore open the envelope, and without relaxing a muscle of his rigidly drawn face, read the epistle through, then here escaped between his set teeth but a single word:

"Entrapped!"

Turning on his heel he walked back to the surgeon, and asked:

"Doctor, how long is it since Miss Merton left?"

"Not quite half an hour."

"Thank heaven! I'm yet in time to save Bertha," he muttered to himself, as he strode away toward his tent. Reaching it, he entered, and taking his pistol and sword from a table, he attached it to his belt, and buckling it on, walked to the entrance way. As he stood leaning against the tent pole he formed a fine manly picture in the evening light, his thick, black wavy hair pushed back from the broad, white brow of his uncovered head, and his tall, full figure clad in a dark blue uniform with its golden buttons across his breast, while on each shoulder gleamed and danced in the uncertain light the golden leaves of a major.

Standing there in the dim, shadowy twilight, oblivious to the noisy hum, and the thousands of expiring camp-fires of the large army—for his thoughts were drifting backward to dear and sad scenes of his boyhood, far across the dark, blue waves—there came over his face a tender sadness, that illuminated it with a nobleness that almost rendered it handsome, were it not for the traces of dissipation there.

But gradually the sadness of his face melted away—like snow on a volcano's peak from the internal fire—and over it came a look of determination, mingled with anger, as he thought:

"So you've crossed my path again, James Sneaker—or John Shackle, as you call yourself now! I think I would have known your handwriting—for it seems engraven on my heart in letters of fire—had you attempted to disguise it, or were my eyes grown dim with years. Your cruel deed started me on the downward path, twenty long years ago! And you, alone, are responsible for the dissipated life I've led! You allured my only sister on to ruin, as fair and noble a girl as ever placed her heart and hand in a villain's care! You betrayed her and left her alone to face a cold and heartless world! She felt her disgrace bitterly, to her very heart's core, and saw but one escape from her shame—in death! So she took the cup of poison and drank it to the dregs! And to-night she sleeps peacefully in her tomb! And when her spirit is wafted beyond the sky, I think the God of all will not judge her too harshly for her only sin!

"But, Shackle, I do not envy you your conscience, or your reckoning with your Creator, when your wicked course is run! You had me thrown into prison when I tried to avenge the dearest and sweetest of sisters—I can see her now, in my wild imagination, and again stroke her dark brown, wavy hair, and watch her liquid black eyes look trustingly. up to mine! Yes, my darling Nelly, I can see your sweet face gazing up from the grave for vengeance! And here, to-night, amid the clash of war, between the contending armies, where there is no perverted justice or judge, we shall meet, and then I shall show you as little mercy as you showed to her!

"You think to have another victim in Bertha Merton, but retribution is close on your track! I'll cleave your wicked body, or else my right hand has lost its cunning, and my steel will refuse to cut! Yes, I'll *thwart* your devilish purpose, or leave another victim for you to gloat over!

"But I must to action, and, ere the day dawns, settle the old score with you!"

With these last thoughts he entered the tent again, and putting on a large black overcoat, which he buttoned across his breast to conceal his uniform, he strode out and walked rapidly through the camp. Reaching and passing the Union pickets without difficulty, he moved rapidly, yet watchfully, toward the cottage. When within about a quarter of a mile of it he suddenly came upon four Confederates kneeling on the ground in a group. They had been making a reconnoissance in front of the Federal lines, and had now fallen back to a more safe distance, out of the range of the pickets' rifles.

Marshall, as he approached them, assumed a bold demeanor, as if he were one of their officers, and cried commandingly:

"Halt! Who goes there?"

They made no reply at first, and seemed inclined to retreat, but after a hurried conference one of them answered:

"Friends!"

"Advance, friends, and give the countersign!"

"Stonewall Jackson!" replied one of the soldiers.

"All right," said Marshall, as he passed onward.

A few minutes after, Marshall reached the cottage garden, and, pushing open the little gate, walked up to the door.

*   *   *   *   *

As Shackle yelled the words, "I'll *ruin you!*" he sprang forward and seized Bertha savagely by the shoulder. When she felt his grasp all hope died within her heart, and a feeling of horror seized her. Almost at that instant a muscular shoulder was thrown against the door, the lock bursted from its fastenings, and as the door swung open, Marshall sprang into the room!

"*Back, villain!*" he cried. "*Back!*"

As he spoke he threw off his overcoat—which he had previously unbuttoned—while his hand, almost involuntarily, grasped his sword.

"*Save me!*" cried Bertha, rushing to him for protection.

He laid his hand gently on her shoulder, as he said calmly, in a low tone: "You are free, my little lady! I'll *attend* to the scoundrel! Now, go back to the camp."

"But he may wound you," she said, hesitatingly.

"No danger of that: I'm too good a swordsman for him!"

She still lingered, and he continued, "Go, Miss Merton. Go! *I'll soon settle with him!* I *want you* to leave."

"Very well," she answered, and left the room.

Shackle stood glaring at Marshall like some wild beast at bay, his face convulsed with rage, while his eyes seemed balls of fire, ready to start from their sockets! For some moments there was a death-like silence, then Shackle hissed between his tightly clenched teeth, with an oath, as he grasped his sword handle almost convulsively:

"Marshall, I'm a dangerous man! *I'll cut your heart out if you don't leave!!*"

An expression of the strongest contempt and defiance crossed Marshall's face, mingled with a sneer, as he said, scornfully:

"*I've courted death too often to have a* SINGLE *fear now!* My God! how I have prayed and waited *for this!*"

At Marshall's words there swept over the villian's distorted face an indescribable expression of fear, while his hand trembled. And as he gazed into the face of the other, and saw there a calm, cold desperation—such as only comes over a man through years of anger, suffering and disappointment—he saw but one chance of escape—that of killing his adversary.

The two men stood watching each other, (like two wild beasts of prey before making a spring) for a few seconds, each waiting for the other to commence the death struggle, then Marshall said, in a calm, icy tone, that rang out sharp and distinct:

"Are you ready? Then defend yourself!"

Instantly their swords crossed with a sharp, metallic ring. Almost the next instant Shackle disengaged his blade and made a thrust *in carte*, which though Marshall skillfully parried, just grazed his arm, tearing the sleeve of his coat.

"Ah!" thought Marshall, "he's a better swordsman than I thought. I must watch him!"

Then their blades crossed again, and for nearly a minute the clash of the steel rang through the apartment, each evidently waiting for the other to make a thrust. At last Shackle grew furious with rage, and stepping slightly backward, then advancing, made a quick, vigorous thrust, which the other parried, instantly giving a counter thrust, just scratching his adversary's arm with the point of the blade.

With an oath of rage, Shackle made a furious thrust, that required all the other's skill and power to parry.

Once more their swords crossed, and for fully a minute and a half their blades clashed, as if in sword-play. Shackle's face was distorted with rage and fear, and his arm trembled, while the other's countenance was calm and determined. One would have thought, to have glanced at it, that he was but playing with his adversary. As the struggle went on Shackle grew more and more furious, for the very calmness of his opponent seemed to urge on his passion.

Finally, he could bear it no longer, and with a wild yell of rage, like a madman, he made a powerful lunge at Marshall. The latter was fully prepared, and, stepping backward, easily parried the thrust, and then springing forward, gave a quick one in return, piercing the other's shoulder. From the wound the hot blood flowed freely, as with a howl more of uncontrollable anger than pain, Shackle leaped backward, knocking over the lamp, and plunging the room in darkness!

The next moment Marshall heard the crash of a breaking window, and Shackle had sprung through it, carrying with him sash and glass. Immediately Marshall started to follow, but as he stepped on the window-sill, he heard two shots in rapid succession, and Shackle fell dead, shot through the heart! Springing upon the ground, Marshall gazed in the direction of the flashes, and saw two men, still grasping their smoking pistols.

In answer to the former's inquiring looks, one of the men raised his lantern, and unbuttoning his coat, showed his badge of authority, as he said:

"We're London detectives. He was a bad 'un! A dangerous cove!"

"Yes, he was," replied Marshall. "I've been amusing him, myself, inside, but it got too hot for him, and he jumped out. But *it seems*, from appearances, that he jumped from the *frying pan* into the *fire!*"

"Yes," replied one of the detectives, smiling grimly. "We've tracked him over half the continent, but we've got 'im at last! But I *tell you!* he was a sharp 'un! Up to all kinds of tricks and deviltry! He got away from us many a time by a close shave! But I think we've made short work of 'im this time!"

The three men knelt down by the prostrate villain and gazed into his face. It was horribly distorted in death, with hatred, rage and fear impressed upon it. And as used to death as these men were, they started back in horror at the awful sight! As one of the detectives said, laconically:

"He's dead!"

And so he was, and Jeremiah Marshall's revenge was complete!

Entering the house again, Marshall took his overcoat from the floor and putting it on, strode out and stood looking at the body.

"We'll take care of him," said one of the detectives. "There's a big reward for him in London, dead or alive!"

"Very well," replied Marshall, as he moved away in the gloom toward the Federal camp.

When he reached the Confederate outpost one of the soldiers cried:

"Halt! Who goes there?"

"A friend."

"Advance, friend, and give the countersign!" cried the Confederate, bringing his gun to a ready.

"Stonewall Jackson!"

"All right. Pass."

Again he pressed forward, till stopped by a picket, who cried:

"Halt! Who goes there?"

"A friend."

"Advance, friend, and give the countersign!"

"It's all right," replied Marshall.

"No, it is not! I have orders to hold you till the arrival of the Corporal of the Guard."

"I am a Federal officer."

"So much the worse for you! You have been communicating with the enemy."

"How do you know?"

"You have been watched, and seen to enter their lines. It is needless to talk further," said the soldier, seeing Marshall hesitate, "my orders are strict. I am compelled to call the Corporal of the Guard."

Then he called out, "Corporal of the Guard, post Number Four!" Then from post to post, along the line, rang, "Corporal of the Guard, post Number Four!" "Corporal of the Guard, post Number Four!"

The Corporal of the Guard came up at a double-quick, with his gun at right-shoulder-shift, and, as he halted, he said:

"Well, what's up?"

"Major Marshall has returned."

"Major, I must arrest you. I have received orders to do so," said the Corporal, as he placed his hand on Marshall's shoulder. And without further parley, Marshall *was a prisoner of war!*

CHAPTER VI.

JUST IN THE NICK OF TIME.

> THERE'S a divinity that shapes our ends,
> Rough hew them how we may.
> —*Shakespeare.*

AROUND a long pine table, in a large tent, were seated thirteen officers, equal or superior in rank to Major Marshall, constituting a general court-martial, that was to try the charges against the latter, that of "holding correspondence with, and giving intelligence to the enemy." These were very serious charges, for, if proven, their punishment, in time of war, was by death. A court-martial during hostilities is entirely a different body in its action from one in time of peace. During tranquility a trial by court-martial may drag along for weeks, even months, before arriving at a decision, but when the army is in active hostilities its action is usually short and decisive. And then again, the punishments meted out are very different; in peace the penalties rarely exceed fine or imprisonment, or, in the case of an officer, dismissal from the service; but during war the punishment is frequently by death. And this is necessarily right, for a soldier or officer may in tranquility give information to outsiders that may make little or no material difference, but which, given in the face of an enemy, may thwart a general's plans, cost the army thousands of men, or even bring upon it defeat or ruin.

The officers of the court-martial were seated at the table according to rank, the president at its head, the judge advocate opposite, and the others on the right and left of the former, beginning at the head of the table with the highest rank. Marshall was seated at the right hand of the judge advocate (the prisoner's place,) while the witnesses were standing at his left.

From the officers' sober faces, and their constrained, hesitating manners —that spoke more than words—one could plainly observe that it was an uncongenial duty for them. And it is nearly always so, for in the army there springs up among the soldiers a strong friendship, particularly in each regiment, but still extending through the entire army, engendered by the very hardships, dangers and scenes of death they have passed through together. But in Marshall's case it was more so, for he, by his good heartedness, genial ways, and his ready, witty remarks and answers, had won a host of friends, some of whom were now members of the court-martial.

The court being called to order, the judge advocate read the order for its assembling, also the charges to be investigated, then followed the question whether or not the prisoner wished to challenge any member.

"No, I do not," replied Marshall, calmly, "I am perfectly satisfied with every officer chosen."

The members of the court were then sworn, followed by the reading of the charges to the prisoner, and the latter's arraignment by the question:

"Major Marshall, you have heard the charges preferred against you; how say you—guilty or not guilty?"

"Not guilty," replied Marshall, and the trial began.

There were three principal witnesses against Marshall, the picket who had arrested him, and two police guards.

One of the latter was the first sworn, and testified that he had had his attention drawn to Major Marshall by seeing him pass their pickets and move directly toward the enemy. His suspicions were aroused, so he followed him, first calling another guard to accompany him. "We approached," the witness continued, "an outpost—or rather scouting party—of the enemy, and after a short parley passed. We could not hear the conversation, as we were too far away, but we supposed he gave their countersign, for the Confederates seemed satisfied. We then notified the proper authority of Marshall's strange action, who ordered the pickets to arrest him if he returned. After this we hid in the darkness, as near the Confederates as we could without attracting their attention. After about three quarters of an hour Major Marshall returned, and as he was passing the enemy's scouts we heard one of them demand the countersign, which he undoubtedly gave, for one of them replied, 'All right, pass.'"

The other police guard now gave his testimony, corroborating that of his comrade.

The sentinel then gave the particulars of the arrest, after which several other witnesses were examined, but their evidence was of little value.

Then, amid an almost breathless silence, Marshall arose and briefly stated his side of the case. But it was evident from his careless manner and words that he had no hopes of acquittal. For from the moment he learned that he had been followed and watched by the guards he yielded to his fate. He stated that his reason for going to the cottage beyond the Federal lines was to rescue a lady friend from a scoundrel, who had decoyed her there by a falsehood about a pretended sick friend. He further said that he had released the lady and become engaged in a duel with swords with her former captor. That the latter, becoming hard pressed, had sprung from the window, but before he could escape he had been mortally wounded by two English detectives, who were searching for him for the crime of murder.

"But who and where was the lady?" the judge advocate asked. She would be an important witness in his favor.

This question he refused to answer unless the court would guarantee that no charges should be preferred against her. But this it did not have the power to promise, as he very well knew. The judge advocate urged and entreated him to reveal the lady's name, but in vain, for in his resolution not to implicate Bertha he remained firm, nobly declaring that if he must suffer, he would not bring her into trouble.

But what had become of the English detectives? suggested a member. They would be excellent witnesses in his favor.

He did not know where they now were, but one of them had informed him that they were going to New York. Concerning them he spoke freely, describing them, giving their names and other particulars. But this information was of no value, for no one knew where they were to be found.

At last, animated by the warm zeal the others had manifested in his favor, Marshall arose and made a brilliant, logical argument in his own behalf. But, taken as a whole, it was a poor defense, and no one knew it better than did Marshall himself.

Then followed the finding of the court, but we shall not go into details, but simply say that, notwithstanding Marshall's weak defense, there were three who voted "Not guilty." They were willing to believe his simple story—implausible as it may have seemed to the others—without asking for further proof. But the other ten members made the necessary two-third vote which is required to determine the conviction of a prisoner, when, as in this case, the law absolutely and without any discretion in the court, condemns him to suffer death.

As the guards led Marshall away, he appeared by far the most calm and unconcerned person present, and when he reached the open air and his old village friends plied him with questions concerning the result, he replied coolly, and with a recklessness so characteristic of the man and the life of danger and vicissitudes he had led for years.

"Well, boys, they've sort of annihilated, kind of Vandalized me!"

Marshall was placed in confinement and closely guarded till the day for the execution arrived, but five days after his sentence.

It was a warm, clear day, toward the close of September; the sky formed a bright blue arch above—except for an occasional white cloud floating here and there—while a warm breeze swept gently along the Shenandoah Valley, giving as yet no signs of the approaching winter, when the somber cortege containing Marshall and his coffin in an ambulance, surrounded by a guard, started for the place chosen for the execution, about half a mile from the camp. Arriving near the spot, Marshall left the ambulance, and walked with a firm step to the ground selected. Here a grave had been dug, and near it was placed the coffin, while Marshall took his place beside it. In front of him stood the firing party, two from each regiment, half of whom were held in reserve, while outside of this was drawn up— forming three sides of a hollow square—the long gleaming lines of an entire division. Near Marshall's right stood a small group of men, and the deep shadow of gloom on their countenances showed that they were more than ordinary observers. They were his old friends from St. Arlyle A few minutes before, each had shaken hands with him and bade him a sad farewell. During his imprisonment they had—led by Charles Landon—made every effort in their power to effect his release, but in vain.

On every face in that huge throng there was a solemn, sober expression, for although amid the shock of battle a soldier may see a comrade fall dead or wounded, and, in his excitement and eagerness to press on to victory, may hardly notice it, yet in his calm moments to see a comrade executed in cold blood savors too much of the feeling that it is murder.

When Marshall had taken his place near the open grave, the provost marshal stepped forward and read the sentence. His voice trembled, while his eyes grew moist, for he and Marshall were old friends! When he finished reading he approached the accused, and as he shook hands with him said sadly, as he brushed away a tear with his coat sleeve;

"Marshall. old friend, this is a hard duty for me to perform! I wish to heaven there was a way to escape it!"

"Never mind, Ned, old fellow," said Marshall, coolly, "you can't help it. So don't take it to heart so."

"I wish from the bottom of my heart," replied the other, "I could help you!"

'Yes, I know you would. Thank you, Ned, my dear fellow, and don't forget the message for my folks across the sea. Farewell!"

"No, I'll not forget it! Goodbye!"

Then the usual question was asked, if he had anything to say why the sentence should not be executed.

He raised his head, and, turning his gaze toward the men, said in a calm, clear voice, without the tremble of a muscle:

"Fellow soldiers, I wish to say but a few words to you. I am satisfied with the decision, for I cannot well see how it could have been otherwise. For events have transpired to seemingly prove my guilt, till it looked as if fate had willed it thus. But through all my life, with all my faults—and I know they are not a few—I have never proved false to the flag I swore to defend! I had hoped that if ever I met death on the field of strife it would be amid the shock of battle, fighting a common foe. For the dearest wish of my heart was that when all was over with me—to have the news sent over to my dear mother, far across the dark blue waves, in Erin's isle, that her son had proved true to the trust reposed in him. But it has been willed otherwise, and I submit! So, comrades, with my friendship to you all and with enmity to none, I bid you a last farewell!"

For several moments after Marshall ceased speaking there was a deathlike silence, and amid it the officer of the firing party stepped forward and drew his sword. Every eye was fixed on the prisoner, as with throbbing hearts and bated breaths they waited, in awful silence, expecting the next moment to see him fall, riddled with bullets, as the officer gave the command: "Ready—Aim——"

At that instant there was confusion in the ranks of the division, attracting general attention, and the next moment they parted and a horseman rode rapidly through the gap and bounded in front of the firing squad! As he reined up his horse he cried: "*Carry—Arms!*"

There was a hesitation of several moments, as the men stood spell-bound, gazing with wonder at the officer, who, with the glittering stars of a major general, had so suddenly appeared before them. Then on many a lip trembled the question: "Who is he?" But as he repeated the command in a clear, ringing voice, there was an indescribable magnetism in it, as they recognized the man whose presence had sent a thrill through them on many a bloody field. *It was General George B. McClellan!*

When the order was obeyed, the General said briefly: "Evidence has been received which entirely exonerates Major Marshall. He will therefore report to his regiment."

Then, turning his horse, the General bounded away, as a cheer broke from the firing squad, which he gracefully acknowledged by raising his hat. This was the signal for a general burst from the division, which grew into a perfect storm of cheers, as he galloped through the line. These were followed by storm after storm of huzzas, till their dashing commander rode out of view.

Meanwhile Marshall stood bewildered with joy, like one in a dream, till the men broke ranks and crowded around him. The first to spring to his side were his village friends, and as Charlie Landon grasped his hand he exclaimed:

"Thank heaven for this! All's well that ends well!"

"Yes," said Marshall, "God moves in His mysterious way, but He does all things for the best!"

Then, as the air rang with cheers, as his comrades almost caught him in their arms, his eyes for the first time grew moist with emotion, that fear had been powerless to effect.

The explanation of Marshall's rescue is soon told. But three days before the time fixed for the execution, Bertha heard of it for the first time. Though it filled her breast with amazement and grief, it did not overpower her, for she resolved to save him. She immediately attempted to see the commander-in-chief. Although several times unsuccessful, she at last, by her womanly, indomitable perseverance, succeeded in accomplishing what his other friends had failed to do. She told her story so simply and with such earnest sorrow that it won the general's favor. But she was not satisfied till she had obtained the evidence of the detectives, who were now in New York. Then the general was satisfied, and with that sense of justice so characteristic of him, immediately sprang on his horse and rode rapidly for the place of execution, where he arrived just in the nick of time.

For about a month after the Battle of Antietam the Army of the Potomac lay encamped on the field, then again came the order to move on to the Confederate capital. On the 26th of October McClellan began to advance, and almost at the same time the Confederates began moving to the same point. It was a grand spectacle—this race between the two great armies; the Union forces on the east side of the Blue Ridge Mountains, and the Confederates on the west, each making every effort to reach Richmond first! And eagerly the whole country watched for the result.

But on the night of the 7th of November occurred an event that thwarted all McClellan's plans. On that night, amid a terrible snow storm, he and General Burnside were seated in the former's tent, when General Buckingham, a messenger from the War Department, arrived and placed in McClellan's hands an order removing him from the command of the army, and appointing Burnside in his place. McClellan read the order without a sign of emotion, then as he gave it to his former lieutenant he said calmly: "Burnside, you command the army."

General McClellan was ordered to report himself at Trenton. In New Jersey, so he immediately made preparations for his departure. That night he issued an address to his troops, full of kindness and regard. And the next day he visited the various camps and reviewed the officers and men for the last time. It was a sad day for the army. For never, perhaps, in the world's history, were men more attached to their commander, and on their leader's part, Cæsar's Gallic legions were not dearer to him nor the army of France dearer to Napoleon than was the Army of the Potomac to McClellan. For he had formed it, and watched it with strongest pride, as it grew in power and perfection. Then, with it he had shared its triumphs and its defeats, till it had grown to be the idol of his heart.

As the General, with his staff, rode rapidly through the ranks, gracefully recognizing and bidding farewell to the men, "the cries and demonstrations of the men (says an officer who was there) were beyond all bounds—wild, impassionate and unrestrained. Disregarding all military forms, they rushed from their ranks and thronged around him, with the bitterest complaints against those who had removed from command their beloved leader."

The next morning McClellan boarded the train for Warrenton When the cars reached the junction—where there were several divisions drawn up in line —a salute from several batteries was fired. Then, as the men caught sight of their former commander on the platform, the wildest enthusiasm prevailed. The cheers and cries were almost deafening, as the men actually rushed from the ranks and crowded around the General, to catch a last glimpse of him and hear his parting words. Amid a lull in the storm of cheers, and just as the train was starting, he stepped to the edge of the platform and said:

"Comrades, I wish you to stand by General Burnside, as you have stood by me, and all will be well. Good-bye."

It was the signal for a wilder burst of cheers than ever, which continued till the train was lost from view.

General Burnside fought the Battle of Fredericksburg, in which the Federal forces were unsuccessful, and then once more the commander of the Army of the Potomac was changed, and General Joseph Hooker became its chief.

CHAPTER VII.

THE BATTLE OF CHANCELLORSVILLE.

"THE sun had set:
　　The leaves with dew were wet;
Down fell a bloody dusk
On the woods that second of May,
Where Stonewall's corps, like a beast of prey,
Tore through, with angry tusk."

SERENELY was drawing to a close a lovely afternoon on the second of May, 1863, amid the green hills and vales along the Rappahannock River, in old Virginia. The sun was setting in all his fiery splendor over the lofty summits of the far away Blue Ridge, bathing them with a rosy hue. The sky above was streaked with streamers of the vividest crimson, whose edges were bordered with waves of gold, that gently faded into the brightest blue. Here and there, amid the sea of azure, rested small white clouds, with just the faintest rosy tinge, like fairy sails lying at anchor on some peaceful ocean's breast.

Away to the west lay the broad waters of the Potomac, gleaming in the fading sunlight, while spreading south-westward from the river were rolling hills and small plains, covered with the greenest carpet of spring-time. Between precipitous bluffs, several miles from the Potomac and nearly parallel with it, ran the Rappahannock River. On the south bank of the river stood the town of Fredericksburg, while back of it arose Marye's Heights, rendered famous, but a few months before, in the Battle of Fredericksburg, when division after division of the Federal army had been hurled again and again, but in vain, against the blazing stone wall near its crest. And now from the same heights gleamed and flashed in the evening sunlight—as if bidding defiance to all beneath—the bright cannons of the Confederates. Forming a line with, and extending from each side of the height, and almost hidden in the ravines and foliage, had lain, the day before, the army of General Lee, 62,000 strong. But during the previous night several divisions of it had marched mysteriously away. Where were they now? We shall soon see—even before the light of this day fades into darkness!

A few miles up the river above Fredericksburg, was the large forest of the Wilderness; and in its midst, in several open glens, in the form of a huge U, with its limbs pointing toward the river, lay the Army of the Potomac. On every side, the army was surrounded by the trees and thick undergrowth of the woods, the only modes of egress and ingress being several narrow roads, which were guarded by artillery and infantry.

There had been skirmishing with the enemy during the day, but the men were now resting. Their arms were stacked, and the soldiers were engaged in cooking their evening meal, as the low hum of their voices sounded over the field. The sun had sunk, till it appeared a great fiery ball in the west. The last beams of day were struggling amid the dark foliage of the forest, while out of it was floating, from the wild flowers and sweet scented climbers, the soft, balmy breath of May.

Suddenly there was a commotion in the forest on the right of the army. Large numbers of birds were frightened from the trees and flew with a shrill cry over the field. These were followed by hundreds of deer, hares, rabbits and other game, which sprang over the works and rushed in wild confusion through the ranks. "What does it mean?" exclaimed the men. But the next moment they were answered by the blast of bugles and a heavy burst of cheers and yells, instantly followed by a deadly storm of bullets. Then they knew that the woods were filled with armed men, and that the terrible "Stonewall" Jackson with 20,000 men had marched around the army and fallen like an avalanche upon their flank! As large numbers of the unarmed and bewildered men fell dead and wounded before the rain of bullets, the assaulting legions, with wild yells, sprang from the forest, and the bloody Battle of Chancellorsville had begun.

As the triumphant Confederates swept over the field, pouring volley after volley upon the bewildered men, the wildest confusion prevailed, as they fled in every direction, not even waiting long enough to pick up their arms. In vain did their officers rush amid the shattered columns and attempt to rally them! It was a rout, not even excelled by that of Bull Run. And when a regiment did halt it was torn to pieces by the merciless fire of the on-rushing host. At last Jackson's corps reached the breastworks near the Chancellorsville House, which were defended by a brigade of infantry, and here a desperate resistance was made, but it lasted only for a short time, for the victorious Confederates were not to be stopped, as with a fearful yell they sprang over the works and crushed the brigade with their superior numbers. The last remnant of the right wing was now shattered, and fled in the utmost disorder. The routed troops had nearly reached Hooker's headquarters, and the on-rush of the fugitives had almost the effect of an invading army. The situation had grown desperate. Something must be done, and done quickly, or the Army is lost. A new line of battle must be formed, so Hooker pushes forward fresh troops. And one of his commanders, Pleasanton, arrives with his artillery at Hazel Grove, just as the demoralized regiments are rushing wildly past. Close behind them are coming, on the double-quick, Jackson's legions, like mighty walls of steel — twenty thousand strong. It is a momentous and critical hour, filled with the fate of an army. General Pleasanton instantly recognizes the desperate situation, as he turns to a Pennsylvania battalion of cavalry, which has just arrived, and cries wildly:

"Major, you must charge the enemy! Save me ten minutes to get my guns ready. Go, Keenan!"

And the brave young officer, as a smile flits over his face, answers:
"I will."

Keenan knows it is a fearful charge, and that he and his brave three hundred will be riding down to certain death. But the young officer—in peace as gentle and soft-hearted as a girl—never hesitates, and as he turns his horse he says, laughingly, "Good-bye!" Then he cries: "Cavalry, charge!" The next instant the three hundred gallant troopers are riding rapidly upon the twenty thousand foes! It is an awful duty before them, but not one of them shrinks from it. On they rush! They cut through the enemy's skirmishers like a tempest, heedless of the score or more saddles that are emptied! And then what an awful sight appears before them! Line after line of Jackson's legions coming at the double-quick, while amid them are gleaming in the moonlight thousands upon thousands of bristling bayonets! But the brave three hundred halt not! and Keenan flings his cap high into the air, and shouts wildly: "Sabres!"

Instantly every sabre leaps high into the air, and the next moment the three hundred horses are spurred, till they leap right into the wall of bayonets! The advancing lines are shocked and retarded for nearly a mile. Then a desperate struggle follows, but it lasts only for a few minutes, then all is over! And the gallant three hundred are lying weltering in their blood, on the field with their dead commander. But ever around their deed will cling a heroic lustre, for as nobly did they fulfill their duty as in that by-gone cycle, on the field at Thermopylæ, did Leonidas and his brave three hundred Spartans, while in defense of their country, fall fighting to a man, against the mighty Persian host of Xerxes. They fell, but their heroic deed will ever live in history as one of the brightest examples of American valor!

Again the Confederate legions are pressing onward. But Keenan and his brave comrades have not fallen in vain! For more than ten minutes have elapsed, and General Pleasanton's cannons are in position, pouring a murderous fire on the advancing foe.

Soon after, other artillery and infantry are added to these, and at last the enemy is checked.

It was now nine o'clock at night. Although the Confederates had been halted, and the heavy firing had ceased, it was but the lull of preparation before a more desperate and bloody struggle; for both sides were hurrying reinforcements to the front. It was at this very time (while forming for the contest) that the Confederates met with a heavy and irreparable loss. Stonewall Jackson, the leader and originator of this brilliant night attack, fell mortally wounded. He was shot—while returning from a reconnoisance—by his own men, who in the moonlight mistook him and his staff for a body of the enemy's cavalry.

Upon the fall of Stonewall Jackson, General Hill assumed command, and a short time after the desultory fire, which had been constantly maintained, burst almost at once, as if by the preconcerted action of both armies, into wild sheets of flame.

This night-battle was a grand, terrible and soul-stirring scene, that in after years never could fade or grow dim in the minds of the soldiers who took part in the ghastly drama of that eventful night! Although it was approaching midnight, it was not dark, for a full moon shed its silvery light over the raging conflict. And on the calm night air, the roar of over a hundred cannons and the thousands of musketry reverberated with awful distinctness; the sky above was ablaze with the lurid flames of the artillery, while on the field, in the flashing light, lay the mangled and bloody bodies of the slain!

Shortly before midnight the firing began to slacken, and soon after ceased. When the sound of the last gun had died away, the men lay down on their arms to rest, but during the few hours that remained before daylight few of them closed their eyes in sleep. For their brains were far too excited by the awful and weird scenes they had just passed through to seek repose. And when their thoughts did wander from the scenes of that eventful Saturday night, they were to many a more happy Saturday night they had spent in the peaceful homes far away.

At daylight the next morning, the battle began by the Confederates under General Stuart—who had taken command after the wounding of General Hill by a shell—seizing a commanding and elevated position near the Chancellorsville House, which the Federals, through a blunder, had abandoned. Stuart, upon seizing this vantage ground, immediately began covering it with artillery, but in doing so, he became engaged with the rear of Hooker's army. This was the signal for the renewal of the battle, and in a few minutes it was raging along the entire line!

But we shall not describe the battle around Chancellorsville, but turn our attention to another part of the field, eleven miles further down the river, where General Sedgewick's corps was stationed, of which the St. Arlyle regiment formed a part. Sedgewick's corps, during the night, had crossed the river and entered Fredericksburg, driving the enemy's skirmishers before them, and were now, at the first beams of day, making preparations to attack the frowning heights of Fredericksburg.

As soon as daylight breaks, a brigade of Sedgewick's men advance up the sloping side of the height. The sun is shining, but a fog hangs over the hillside, and as the men advance beneath it, on that calm Sabbath morning, a host of sad memories are flooding through their brains, of another day, a few months before, when they charged the frowning heights again and again till the glacis was covered with their dead and wounded comrades, but, alas! in vain!

All is still as death, until they have almost reached the stone wall near the hill's crest, then there is a wild burst of flame, a deafening roar and a terrible shower of iron and lead is hurled through their ranks! Repeatedly they attempt to carry the breastworks, but their ranks are thinned and torn asunder by the merciless fire, and they are forced to fall back, leaving the ground covered with their dead and wounded.

But ere long, they are rallied again, at the foot of the hill, and, being heavily reinforced, once more advance to the attack.

In the center of the attacking column has been placed the St. Arlyle regiment.

The men as they press forward, meet with a light fire, till within about four hundred yards of the wall, then the guns on the hill pour a terrific volley of canister and grape upon them, tearing huge gaps in their ranks, but they bravely close the breaches and press onward at a run. Charlie Landon is wounded in the arm, but he is cheering his men on, heedless of the storm of death. And near him is Marshall, who has all the while been conspicuous for his bravery. Each moment the fire grows heavier, the air is filled with deadly missiles, but on the men rush, though the ground is covered with their slain. * At last the stone wall is reached, and regardless of the withering fire, the Federals leap over it and drive the enemy from their position.

Among the first to vault over the wall are Landon and Marshall, but as the latter reaches the ground he is struck in the breast by a bullet, but ere he falls Charlie Landon catches him in his arms. And as Landon lays him tenderly on the ground the wounded man says:

"Leave me. Colonel. They want you up there!" waving his hand toward the hill's crest.

"My poor fellow, it's hard to leave you so, when perhaps you are bleeding to death, and I could help you," said Charlie, sadly, as he looked down tenderly into the wounded man's face. "But duty forces me onward, and I suppose I must obey," he continued, as he reluctantly placed the other's head on a knapsack for a pillow. And as he arose, hesitatingly, there was a desperate struggle going on in his tender heart, between pity and duty.

"Yes, leave me, Colonel; they need you up there."

"I suppose I must! But it is bitter to do so!"

The regiment had already passed them, and there was not a moment to lose, for already the men were looking for their leader, so Charlie said hurriedly yet tenderly, as he quickly applied a wet pledget, covered with tannic acid, to the wound, "My dear fellow, I'll be back to you the moment the struggle is over. Good-bye!"

"Thank you, my boy! Good-bye!" said the wounded soldier, calmly, as the other bounded away.

The stone wall and the rifle-pits have been captured and cleared, but the cannons on the hill are still vomiting with renewed thunder their shot and shell! But up the brave fellows go, though their ranks are cut through and through. But nothing can daunt the courage and enthusiasm of these heroic men! At last the hill top is reached, and amid wild cheers the batteries are taken. And in a few moments more the stars and stripes are floating proudly on the crest!

After capturing the Heights, the Federals pursued the enemy for nearly two miles; but the Confederates being strongly reinforced, they were compelled to halt. But the brilliant charge of Sedgewick's men in carrying the Fredericksburg Heights was in vain, for through several blunders in other parts of the field, the battle had been already lost. But this brave charge will ever "shine out as the one relieving brightness amid the gloom of that hapless battle."

So during Tuesday night, amid a violent rain storm, and after three days of fighting, the Army of the Potomac crossed the river on pontoon bridges, and the great battle of Chancellorsville was ended!

AT REST AT LAST.

SOLDIER, rest! thy warfare o'er,
Dream of fighting field no more;
Sleep the sleep that knows not breaking,
Morn of toil or night of waking.
—*Scott.*

AFTER the battle of Chancellorsville, the Army of the Potomac fell back to its old camping ground at Falmouth. Here the thousands of wounded, who had fallen in the battle, had been conveyed across the river, filling the numerous hastily improvised hospitals to their utmost capacity.

Near the outskirts of the town, in a small rose-wreathed cottage, with a cool, inviting ivy-twined porch, facing a little garden, redolent with blooming flowers, Marshall's St. Arlyle friends had tenderly carried the wounded soldier. Though his wound was a severe and painful one, it was not necessarily fatal. Almost from the first, all that medical skill could do for him had been done, for Dr. Granville and Charles Landon had been persistent in their attention to him. Bertha had also hurried to his side, and all that lay in the power of a woman's gentle hand to perform for a wounded soldier—and that is more than words can tell—she eagerly did for him. For she felt that she owed him an inestimable debt of gratitude for his noble services on that eventful night when she had been allured to the lonely house near the enemy's lines. And Marshall's conduct afterward, when arrested, in refusing to criminate her, though thereby he could have gained a most important witness in his defense, had ennobled him in her estimation, with martyr-like qualities.

On the fifth day after receiving his wound he seemed to be doing well, when suddenly one of the ligated arteries broke and bled so profusely that it required the combined efforts of Dr. Granville and Charlie Landon to control the hemorrhage. After the ruptured artery had been "taken up" he fell into a gentle sleep, and Bertha, who had been constantly by his side, left him to attend to others. But as soon as she was at leisure she eagerly returned to him.

He had just awoke, and was very pale and weak. After she had given him a stimulant, in answer to her question of how he felt, he looked up vaguely, as if his thoughts were wandering far away, while he said sadly, yet still with a shade of the old peculiar humor on his pale face:

"Sort of annihilated; kind of Vandalized."

In spite of her heavy heart, a faint smile crossed her lips at this characteristic reply.

He saw it and his pallid face brightened with something of the old humor as he said:

"I've uséd those words so long and often that they have almost become a part of my nature. But I have no doubt they are not far from the truth now."

"I hope not," she said, sincerely.

"Yes," he said, calmly, "I have a presentiment that this is the last of earth for me; that my bark of life is surely and rapidly sailing into the port of eternity!"

"Cheer up," she replied, "for while there's life there's hope. God often gives us dark hours, so that we may fully appreciate the bright sunshine He sends at last!"

"True, but I think my sunshine will be in another world!"

That night he slept well and awoke refreshed. And his friends became much encouraged, thinking he was on the way to recovery.

From the day he had rescued Bertha he had become a changed man. Since then he had not drunk a drop of liquor; the old aimlessness fled, and he grew more thoughtful and eager to redeem the past. He was not less brave, but he tried to be nobler and better.

For several days he seemed to grow stronger, but one morning there came suddenly a rapid change for the worse, and it became evident that his end was approaching. One afternoon he called Dr. Granville to his side and asked:

"Doctor, it is all over with me, is it not?"

Dr. Granville replied, sadly, "your case is very critical, but there is a feeble chance for life."

He turned inquiringly to Landon, as Charlie replied:

"Yes, it is a desperate case. But you are in God's hands, you know. Let us hope for the best."

"Thank you, Doctor, my boy; I understand. And I am willing to go. For I think, now at last, I'm able to say, what I ought to have learned to say years ago: what is God's will is mine. For He does all things for the best, though His ways may not always be plain to us. But the good Book tells us: 'It is the glory of God to conceal a thing.' And it is, no doubt, best for us not to know His mysterious ways of kindness."

"I've courted death before," he continued, "a hundred times and more, but it has passed me by. And now, when I've commenced to lead a better life, I'm called to go. But perhaps our Heavenly Father, in his sweet mercy, calls us when we're at our best. In my poor case, infinitely far from what I ought to be. But in the future I had hoped to retrieve something of my wasted life—at least do better. But man proposes, and God disposes. And I can't help thinking, always for the best."

Throughout the afternoon and evening the hemorrhage continued, and late in the night, as he grew weaker and weaker, his mind began to wander to other scenes, to other days, when in the voyage of life he was but a boy, and when hope and young vigor pictured the future with the bright sunshine and happiness that only youth can cherish!

As Charles Landon and Frank Meredith watched by his bedside they often caught the name of his sister trembling upon his lips, around whose memory such a wealth of his love was clasped. He saw her again in her girlhood, in all of her beauty, sweetness and innocence; and his thoughts of her were ever thus, to the last.

Then his mind wandered to the after days of his erratic career. In his thoughts he was again in Turkey, mingling amid its fields of blood and death! Once more the scene was changed, and he was sharing the fate of down-trodden Greece. Again the drama of his life was varied, and he was acting over his checkered course in Germany. Another turn of fortune's wheel, and he was amid Mexico's turbulent strife again. But wherever his thoughts wandered, there were always kind words and wishes for many a name of those whose friendship he still remembered.

Then, as his mind drifted into later years and the actors and scenes shifted again—in his fancy he was living over his life in St. Arlyle. And by his mutterings they learned that many happy memories of his bygone life were linked around the little village he never more would see. And as he named over his village friends, one by one, for not a name was omitted or forgotten, the remembrance of each struck a tender chord in his heart.

There were two names he often repeated in his mind's wanderings, and always with the strongest solicitude and praise. They were those of Bertha and Charles. Bertha he frequently mentioned as the little curly-headed child he had watched grow into the beautiful girl.

Of Charlie he often murmured words of strong admiration, but it seemed to pain and perplex him to think that so brave and generous a fellow could be untrue to Bertha.

And now, for the last time, his thoughts changed, for the drama of his life was almost ended—and in his fancy he was following again the fortunes of the Army of the Potomac; fighting over the bloody battles of the Peninsular campaign; mingling again amid the strife of Antietam; again struggling through the carnage of Fredericksburg. And ere the curtain of his fancies fell he lived over that bloody and fatal day when his regiment charged up the glacis, under the fire from the Fredericksburg Heights, on the battle field of Chancellorsville!

His mutterings ceased, and for some time he lay in silence; then his head moved slightly and he awoke perfectly rational. Charles arose and went to his bedside, when he asked for a drink of water. After drinking it he turned his eyes toward Meredith, whose head was bent down on his arms, and asked, in a whisper: "Is he asleep?"

"Yes," replied Landon.

"Bend your head down, my boy!" said he, "I wish to say a few words privately to you. I wish you to promise to be always a friend—a true friend, in the strongest, purest and best sense of the word—to Bertha. For she is a sweet, generous girl, with the truest, noblest heart that ever beat in a woman's breast. She has a great, heroic soul, as far above envy and greed as the heavens are above the earth. In her many deeds of kindness she realized in all its grandest sweetness, 'What a woman true may be.'"

"Your request is an easy one to grant," replied the young fellow, as a blush mantled his cheek and a tender light filled his eyes, "for she is a noble girl, with a heart as sweet and pure as that of a child. And often when I have stood amid a group of soldiers, when she passed, and I have seen them raise their caps and heard them speak almost reverentially of her many deeds of kindness, as I gazed upon her spiritual beauty, I could almost see a seraphic halo around her beautiful head. And often in my dreams I have seen her as an angel, floating above my rude bed, on many a field of strife. How dearly I love her no words can express. And I can only say, may heaven deal with me, as I deal with her!"

"I am satisfied," said Marshall. "Good night." And he turned his head over on the pillow and soon fell asleep.

It was late the next morning when Marshall awoke. Bertha had just entered the room, and as she gazed down at him she noticed how pale his face had grown, and how weakly he breathed, although his eyes looked unusually dark and bright. She bent over him and asked him how he had slept. At the sound of her voice he turned his gaze toward her in silence, while a shadow of the old merry smile played on his lips, as if the sight of her tender and beautiful face awoke pleasant memories. He remained silent for several moments, watching her face, as if fascinated by its tender beauty, then replied:

"Very well, indeed."

"I'm glad you've rested well," she said, kindly.

"Yes," he replied, "Heaven is always good to us in the end, and gives us rest! That lesson of trust and peace many of us ought to have learned before. And it seems strange to me now that I could not look through the mist of life's troubles and trials, to the better and purer home of tranquility; the rest God has so freely promised to all.

"For these long years I've led a reckless, erring life. But I think and hope that it was more through thoughtlessness than intentional wickedness. I began those years wrong, with not enough of faith and hope, but with a burning desire for revenge, and an utter lack of trust in man—and, I'm afraid, in God also—that finally grew into recklessness!

"But," he added, "there were days in those wild years of recklessness when I tried to throw off the wild life, and I thought I had succeeded, when a mere incident would bring back the old agonizing sorrow of that evening I never could forget! The evening when we learned the truth of my sister's awful death. That tragic scene can never be effaced from my memory. I see it now, as I have seen it many times through all these years! My sister had been keeping company with Shackle for some time—he was a handsome man then, though when you knew him you would hardly believe it, so greatly was he changed—when we learned he was already married. But, on seeking my sister, we found she had fled. My father sent messengers in every direction to seek her. Meanwhile we were in terrible suspense. At last one of the messengers found her, and brought us the truth. I shall never forget the scene that then occurred. It was evening, and my mother, my father (who was just recovering from a severe attack of pneumonia,) and I were standing on the porch when the messenger came. He informed us that he was too late; and that my sister had committed suicide by taking poison. Then followed an awful spectacle, that through all the after years has never grown dim! My mother, with a terrible scream, fell fainting on the door step ere any one could catch her. My father turned deadly pale, while he pressed one hand upon his breast, as if to control his agony. Then I saw his lips were red, and the next instant the hot blood spurted over his bosom. But ere he fell we caught him and carried him into the house. He lingered on, but never recovered from the shock. He died a month after— while I was far away in Turkey. I was at first stunned by the awful news; my heart seemed to stop beating, and I staggered like a drunken man; then tears came to my relief. Then I cursed Shackle with the bitterest anathemas my tongue could utter, and I swore vengeance should be mine.

"I went to his house and inquired for him, but was spurned from the door Then, there in the street, I cursed him again and again, with all the bitterness of my soul. I went home. They had just brought my sister's body and laid it upon a bed. And as she lay there in death's cold embrace, in all her wondrous beauty, her image has ever been impressed upon my mind, through all these after years. She had on the same white dress she had worn before her death; not even the white rose had been removed from her breast, where she had placed it, while one cold little hand was lying beside it, as if she had but just ceased toying with it. Her dark, curly hair clustered around her pale brow and hung far down over her shoulders; the white eyelids were closed, hiding forever the large, lustrous eyes, and her lips were gently parted, as if in sleep.

"I was wild with grief, and in my madness I challenged Shackle to fight a duel. He had me arrested, but my friends soon procured bail for me. I was never prosecuted, for before the day of trial came Shackle fled!

"Two days after my sister's death she was buried. I stood by her grave till I saw the last shovelful of earth thrown in. Then I realized that I had lost her forever! The idolized sister, to whom my heart had been so closely bound. From that moment I became wild and reckless, and I felt I should never know peace and hope again! I only thought and dreamed of vengeance! I lost faith in man, and, I'm afraid, in God too! My heart became steeled to danger. I feared nothing—not even death. I went to Turkey, because there was war there, and I loved turmoil and strife, for the danger and excitement made me forget my grief. I was the leader in many dangerous expeditions. I even courted death over and over again, but I always escaped unscathed. My reckless daring won me rapid promotion, but ere long my ever restlessness urged me onward. I went to Greece, but my sorrow went with me and would not let me rest. Here, amid the battle fields of Greece, I grew, if possible, more reckless and daring than ever. I learned to love danger in its wildest forms. Nothing daunted me, and the men under my command thought I did not know what fear was, or that I was mad. Perhaps I was. I was trying to drown my sorrow, but it clung to me like the Old Man of the Sea did to Sindbad the Sailor. My fearlessness won me promotion. I was on the road to fortune But it was the same ending. The old restlessness came back with treble its former force, and I flung everything aside and fled to Germany. But, as ever, my grief went with me.

"I had been in Germany several months, and I was stopping at a hotel in Berlin, when one warm evening as I was walking along the hall of the hotel, I saw a bedroom door partly open and I casually glanced in. There was a man lying on the bed, and I knew him in an instant, in spite of his changed appearance. *It was Shackle!*

"I entered the room and stood leaning over his bed. He was so terribly changed that even I was shocked at the emaciated, haggard, and wild, haunted expression of his countenance. In fact, so awfully was he changed that I would not have recognized him had not his face been constantly before my mental view. If his face was any criterion, he must have suffered terribly. But for him there was no room for pity in my heart. I recrossed the room, and, locking the door, returned and stood leaning over him, as I drew a dagger from my breast.

" 'Vengeance! Vengeance at last is mine!' I thought, as I stood gloating over him. 'You shall not escape now. I can kill you with as little feeling as I would a wild beast! I have hoped and longed for this! And at last it has come! You must die like a dog!' I raised the dagger to bury it in his body. It was already descending in the air, when I suddenly felt a hand grasp my arm! I turned my head, and *there was my sister standing by my side!* Exactly as I had last seen her, on the day of her death—in a white dress, her dark, curly hair clinging about her pale, sweet face, and hanging far down her shoulders, while one little hand was grasping the white rose on her breast. I was struck dumb and I almost fainted, while unconsciously and seemingly by some power stronger than my own, I replaced the dagger. As I did so, a smile of approval crossed her lips, and the next moment she melted into air. I left the room, and fled from the city—away from temptation.

"I'm not superstitious, but I shall always think I saw my sister's spirit standing by my side. I know that physicians account for these supernatural apparitions by telling us: That in such cases either the brain, the retina or the optic nerve being unusually excited, are thus rendered sensitive to an appearance that in reality does not exist. For there is such a close union between the senses and the mind, that we continually transfer to the real world—without being aware of it—that which pertains to the realm of thought. Thus, they say, a picture that has made a deep impression upon us at one time, will reappear to us during partial sleep, perfect in every detail, or, perhaps, varied by the capricious wanderings of our thoughts. And that passion and other strong, violent mental feelings are apt to evoke optical delusions. But, nevertheless I shall always believe I saw her spirit, and that she came in her spirit form to save me from committing murder!

"From the day I saw her sweet spiritual face there came a change for the better—there was more of peace in my heart. Not a full peace, but a touch of tranquility. I endeavored to throw off the old reckless and dissipated habits, but I could not fully succeed. They had gained too strong a hold upon me. But still there were times when my heart was nearer peace than it had known for many years before.

"When I left Germany I went to Mexico. Of the life I led among its wild, revolutionary scenes, I shall not dwell. Then I went to St. Arlyle. Of my life there you are fully familiar. At last the Civil War broke out. I was a soldier, and it seemed but natural that I should enlist, besides, my heart was not yet tranquil enough, but that I still loved strife and excitement, and then, I had truly learned to love the Republic—the grandest example of liberty and justice the world ever saw, or, perhaps, ever will.

"The night Shackle decoyed you into his power," he continued, "I went to the hospital to look for you. There I was given the letter you had left for me. I recognized in a moment that it was Shackle's handwriting, and I knew that he was again at his old villainy. And I determined to save you, let it cost what it would. How I followed you, how I fought Shackle, and how I was afterward arrested, you are fully acquainted.

"The night of my arrest," he continued, after gasping for breath, "as I lay sleeping in the guard house, I suddenly awoke, and there, by my bed-side stood my sister's spirit, exactly as I had seen her once before; her dark hair clustering around her pretty face and hanging over the shoulders of her white dress, while one little hand was grasping the white rose on her breast. She raised her hand and pointed upward, as a sweet smile crossed her lips ere she melted away. Then I knew I had her approval in foiling Shackle's villainy. From that moment there came into my heart a feeling of rest and peace, that I had yearned for through many a weary year. And I felt that the old restlessness had fled and in its stead a sweet tranquility had come! From that day I quit drinking, and I tried to lead a better life. And I hope I have not wholly failed."

"I'm sure you've succeeded," said Bertha, warmly.

The dying soldier was silent for some time, gasping for breath. Then he began in a feeble voice:

"Last night, just before I fell asleep, I saw my sister's spirit standing by my bed. She appeared exactly as she had done twice before—in a white robe, her dark hair hanging about her face and neck, while one small hand was clasping the white rose on her breast. But there was a light on her face I had never seen before—a heavenly light, that shed a pure, sweet radiance into my soul. She raised her hand and pointed upward, as she had done once before. But instead of fading away, as before, she floated upward, far, far away through clouds and space, till I saw her join the angels on the heavenly shore. Then I knew she had pointed and shown me the way. And then my heart, at last, had found the perfect peace and love."

He was rapidly growing weaker, and it was evident that in a few minutes all would be over, as he said, feebly:

"Miss Bertha, I want you to write to my mother, and tell her I fell in defense of the flag I learned to love best of all. Tell her that I died at peace with my God and man. Tell her that ere my life or hers was done, I had hoped to meet her once again in the old home across the water, in Erin's isle. But it has been willed otherwise, and I submit! Tell her I at last found the faith she taught me at her knee. The grand, glorious faith God has given to us all. And tell her that through it I hope to meet her on the shining shore of peace!"

When he ceased speaking he lay motionless, his eyes closed, and he breathed imperceptibly, while a deathly pallor covered his face. But after several moments he slightly rallied, as she bent her ear down to catch his dying words, he said:

"I had hoped, in future years, to lead a better life. The past one was full of care and unrest. But it was my own fault that I found the thorns and missed the roses. But then I'll not complain. The greatest crown of all has been a diadem of thorns! And through it, I hope, I've found the right path up to God; the right way home to peace!"

Then over his face came a sweet expression of tranquility; the rest he had longed for through many a weary year; and the soldier of fortune had crossed the dark ocean into the haven of Eternal Rest!

*　　　*　　　*　　　*　　　*

Of the ill-starred life Marshall led, how shall we judge! We, who know so little of the emotions and struggles of the human heart. For often beneath a calm face is hidden the terrible agony of a bitter sorrow for loved ones, over whom the grass has grown green; yet around whose memories grim spectres of the past will rise to haunt even their brightest moments.

Thus in the breasts of all of us, at times, will come welling up memories haunted by spectres of many shattered hopes, many sorrows, many errors and vain regrets, that will often make us waver or stray from the beaten path.

So, only God can fathom the motives that prompt and direct the actions in each human heart; and, therefore, He alone can estimate the guilt and the sin.

CHAPTER IX.

THE BATTLE OF GETTYSBURG.

   AND backward now and forward
    Wavers the deep array;
  And on the tossing sea of steel
   To and fro the standards reel,
  And the victorious trumpet peal
   Dies fitfully away.
       — *Macauley.*

BEAUTIFULLY the morning of the first of July, 1863, broke over Gettysburg; not a cloud obscured the clear blue sky, while the warm air and streaming sunshine bathed in all its summer splendor the little town soon to be rendered immortal, as the field not only of the most decisive and bloody battle of the Civil War, but as the theatre of one of the greatest conflicts of modern times. From early dawn the scene in the little town had been one of mighty martial splendor and beauty, yet inspiring terror, as the Army of the Potomac passed through it toward the west, with its long blue columns of infantry, their bands playing lively strains and their gay banners floating out on the morning air, while their bright arms flashed and danced in the sunlight with a dazzling splendor; its platoons of cavalry, with gleaming sabres, followed by its batteries of artillery, their huge guns darting back the sun-rays, as if bidding defiance to every foe, while amid its legions rode the crimson-sashed officers, the gold and silver insignia of rank glittering on their shoulders.

As the morning wore away, with a steady tread the serried ranks of the Army of the Potomac moved through the town. It was a few minutes past nine o'clock, when, in the distance, toward the west of the town, a puff of white smoke ascended into the clear, blue sky, and the next instant the crash of musketry rolled into the streets, followed by the heavy report of a cannon. "Crash! crash! boom! boom!" and in a few minutes the crash has grown into a continuous crash, and the boom into a mighty roar.

There had been a sudden collision between the Federal General Buford's regiments, drawn up in line across the Chambersburg road, and an advancing division under General Harry Heath, of Lee's army, and the Battle of Gettysburg had begun.

In a few moments the scene in the town was changed; the terrible roar of the heavy guns had broken the spell. The idlers in the streets who were watching the passing troops turned at the first sound of the guns, and gazed with excited and frightened faces toward the direction of the rapidly increasing roar, and where the puffs of white smoke above the trees told that the battle was raging. Through the serried ranks of the moving army there rolled a gentle ripple of excitement, but it soon increased until it resembled great waves on some ocean's breast. Then followed a grand, exciting scene, as the infantry, with flashing arms and streaming standards, pressed forward at the double-quick, and the cavalry, with clashing and gleaming sabres, galloped rapidly by, while the artillery horse broke into a rapid trot, as the heavy guns thundered along, and even the bands struck up wilder strains, while the drummers loudly rattled their drums, as the trumpeters sent forth their shrill, piercing notes, while, above the din, the officers yelled their orders at the top of their voices, and every order was: "Forward! Forward to the front!"

As the troops rushed forward to the vortex of death, there were no cheers, no bravado, only the fixed lips and determined faces of the men showed the gazers, as they passed, that they knew the bloody work they had to do, and that they intended to do it. And through the beholder there ran an awful shudder, as he thought many of them must meet a terrible death, mangled by shot and shell.

It was the intention neither of General Mead, nor Lee, to fight the battle at Gettysburg, but so rapid had been the movements of both armies that each commander was in ignorance of the whereabouts of the other's troops, until the morning of the battle. General Lee had intended reaching Chambersburg before giving battle, and Mead advanced his left wing under General Reynolds, in front of Gettysburg, as a feint to divert the enemy's attention, while he formed a strong line with his main body behind Pipe Creek, twenty miles distant. Buford, when he found his men in collision with the Confederates, resolved to hold the enemy in check until the arrival of his chief, General Reynolds, who, with his command, was two miles distant.

Reynolds, on his arrival, had no orders from General Mead to commence the battle, but the exigencies of the situation supplied the place of commands. He also saw the necessity of rapid action, as Buford's men were sorely pressed, and on the point of breaking; so, forming his entire command at the edge of the woods, he suddenly charged to Buford's aid. He and his men were met with a perfect storm of bullets, and while gallantly leading forward, General Reynolds fell mortally wounded from his horse, dying where he fell. Notwithstanding the fall of their commander, the men pressed bravely onward with such impetuosity that they drove two Confederate regiments into a railroad excavation, and captured them, with their battle flags.

Reinforcements rapidly joined both combatants, and the battle raged with terrible fierceness, the roar of the artillery was terrific, the wild flashes of flame leaped everywhere amid the sulphurous smoke, like forked lightning, and solid shot and bursting shells were falling in every direction, while the air was filled with bullets.

It was now three o'clock, the heat was intense, and the contest was raging fierce and wild, when, toward the north-east, a long, waving line of gray appeared in view. The new troops were Stonewall Jackson's old legions, hurrying to the field, to decide the fate of the day. Reaching the York road, they debouched into the woods, and with their old, wild, battle cry, fell with crushing force upon the Federal right. The National soldiers, though outflanked and taken in the rear, changed front and fought with the utmost bravery, but the fire poured upon them was terrific—for men who had fought in all the former great battles of the war said they never were under a hotter fire. At last the Federals began to fall back, slowly at first, then more rapidly, till finally their ranks were broken and the retreat became a rout, and they were driven through the streets of Gettysburg in wild confusion, with the loss of five thousand prisoners. The Confederates took possession of the town, and the Federals fell back on their reserve body, which had been posted on Cemetery Hill, behind Gettysburg. It was at this time—as the retreating men were pouring through Gettysburg toward the Hill—that General Hancock arrived on the field. He had been sent by General Mead—who was still at Taneytown, 13 miles distant—to take command, as soon as Mead learned of the battle and the death of Reynolds.

Hancock was very popular with the rank and file of the Army of the Potomac, and his commanding appearance, with his winning, magnetic manner, added to his dashing gallantry, did much toward rallying and forming them into a new line. And it was not long before he had the remnant of the army re-formed on Cemetery Heights, behind ledges, stone walls and bowlders, presenting an abatis of bristling bayonets. Though order had been restored, and a strong front presented toward the enemy, the Federal forces were yet in imminent danger, for it was evident they could not resist successfully a combined attack of the enemy—and defeat meant *ruin!*

It was yet several hours before sunset, and a cloud of Confederate skirmishers were already breasting the hill, when to the astonishment and heart-felt joy of the Federals, they were suddenly recalled, and thus ended the first day of the Battle of Gettysburg. Though it had been a day of terrible carnage, yet bloodier days were to follow. And that night General Lee made a fatal mistake when he did not complete his victory and drive the Federals from their stronghold, for by sunrise the next morning, most of Mead's men had arrived, and the Heights of Gettysburg were covered with the infantry and artillery of the great Army of the Potomac.

* * * * *

The morning of the second of July, 1863, broke over Gettysburg, calm and still; the sun in all its brightness shone through a clear, azure sky, except for an occasional white cloud that floated ominously above, as if predicting the terrible storm of human wrath that would sweep over plain and hill ere the sunset flushed the west. All night long, on the heights above the town, had been arriving the reinforcements of the Federal army, and as the first beams of day gilded with roseate hues the Heights, they fell upon the lines of polished steel—consisting of nearly a hundred thousand men.

In front of the National army, and across a small valley—not more than a mile and a half distant—was formed the Confederate forces, in the shape of an immense crescent, nearly five miles in length, and numbering over ninety thousand men. Viewed by the Federal soldiers on the Heights, they formed a magnificent spectacle, as their long, gray lines stood there in grim battle-array, with their bright arms flashing in the July sunlight, almost as far as the eye could see, while the black mouths of their cannons, that thickly dotted the eastern slope of the hill, frowned ominously up across the vale.

Thus the two armies met, on the 2d of July, in this magnificent amphitheatre at Gettysburg, to decide the fate of the Southern Confederacy.

During the morning there had been some skirmishing, but as the day wore away all became calm. There was a balmy sweetness in the summer air, enhanced by nature's sweet repose. And as the glances of those on the Heights fell beneath, they were entranced by the green-leafed woods, the flourishing orchards, the yellow ripening grain and the verdant meadows, on whose breasts the cattle were feeding, or lying in the shade of the trees, or drinking from the silver-hued streams that rippled along. It was a scene of Nature's sweet repose, but soon to be changed by the wrath of man into scenes of wild turbulence and horror, to fill the air with shrieks of agony, and with the mighty roar of destruction; to cover vale and hillside with the mangled bodies of the slain, and to crimson those silver-hued streams with human blood. For the soldiers soon to be actors in this terrible drama of death were no longer the raw recruits who began the war, but men whom three years of experience with danger, blood and death had taught the awful duties of soldiers, and they had learned those lessons well ere this, on many a blood-stained field!

Shortly after three o'clock there fell over the field an awful calm, sublime in its very oppressiveness, as, with bated breaths and fluttering hearts, the men of these two great armies—in mighty, grand battle-array—awaited the conflict!

It was few minutes of four o'clock, when a Confederate artillery officer waved his sword in the air, and as the blade flashed in the afternoon's waning sunlight, there came a mighty roar from over a hundred guns, massed on the eastern slope of the hill. The cannon balls arched over the little valley and fell with a crash on the sides and summit of the Heights, as they bounded from bowlder to bowlder. The next moment the Federal lines above were swept by a billow of flame, and a hundred and fifty guns hurled back defiance.

The roar of the artillery was terrific, the air was filled with solid shot and bursting shells, and the sulphurous smoke rolled in huge volumes over the field, while amid it darted the red flames from the cannons' mouths.

But all this was but the prelude for more desperate and deadly work.

Partly under cover of the smoke of their guns, the Confederates were seen rapidly forming in line, and in a few minutes more Longstreet's entire corps, nearly one third of the army, was pressing forward at the double-quick to storm the Federal position, while the Confederate artillery, with renewed thunder, poured volley after volley over the advancing men's heads. Down the slope, three lines deep, the men in gray press, then up the glacis toward the Federals they rush, as their lines flash with the fire of their rifles, and in a few minutes more, with wild yells and cheers, they fall with tremendous and savage fury on the Federals.

The battle now raged furiously, and every minute grew wilder and bloodier, till at last it resembled a tempest-tossed sea of destruction. The Confederates poured a close, heavy fire, the stone walls and ledges literally blazed with musketry, and the bullets fell like showers of rain, while over two hundred cannons dealt forth death and destruction on every side! Thus the battle raged all along the line. Cemetery Ridge was a sheet of fire; on Culps Hill both sides charged and counter-charged with demon-like fury; but on the semi-circle about Little Round Top the scene of blood and destruction was grand, terrific and awful! Every inch of air seemed to be alive with bullets, balls and bursting shells; the hillsides were piled with dead and wounded, yet the desperate men charged and re-charged across the blood-stained ground and vale of death!

Thus for more than two hours the earth shook and trembled as if an earthquake had rumbled through its depths, the thunder of the artillery, the crash of the musketry was deafening, and the sulphurous smoke swept in heavy volumes over the field, and, ascending toward the sky, formed a thick canopy above, as if endeavoring to hide from Heaven the scenes of infernal horror beneath, and in the dense smoke the men fought as if in a fog, while the red flames from the cannons darted about amid it, like wild tongues of fire from some demoniacal abyss!

Thus the tempest of death and destruction raged, till the last beams of day faded, and darkness shrouded the field. Even then, though the main body of the Confederate Army had fallen back, yet still between their advanced skirmishers and the Federals, who were resting on their arms, the fire was almost continuous throughout the night.

CHAPTER X.

THE CLOSE OF THE BATTLE OF GETTYSBURG.

"TWICE Hath the sun on their conflict set,
And risen again, and found them grappling yet."

EVEN as early as four o'clock in the morning the desultory fire of the night increased almost at once into sheets of flame, and immediately a terrible struggle followed. Ere long the contestants became so intermingled that it became almost impossible to use the artillery, for fear of killing friend as well as foe. As the battle progressed the air became filled with dust and smoke, and as the sun mounted higher and higher the heat became intense. The Confederates charged again and again with the utmost bravery, but with little effect, for they were pitted against men as courageous and determined as themselves.

Through those long, early hours of morning the fighting was desperate and severe, and the carnage was fearful. That part of the field after the battle was literally bathed with blood, and thickly covered with the bodies of the slain—the blue and gray uniforms mingled in one heap—showing the terrible nature of the determined struggle.

Late in the morning there was a short calm in the storm of battle. Then suddenly there was a mighty burst of cheers and yells from thousands of Confederates, and Ewell's fresh men rushed up the hill and fell with tremendous fury on the National lines. They met with a desperate and stubborn resistance from the Federals, and a hand to hand struggle followed. But at last the Federals were forced from their works, and on rushed the victorious Confederates. But as they approached a stone wall, the men in blue of an entire division arose before them like an apparition, and poured upon them a close, heavy volley. They were mowed down like grain before the sickle, and even these brave warriors could do no more than retreat.

* * * * *

It was noon, and the last sounds of the conflict had several hours before died away. The morning sky, which had been partly hidden by clouds, had now cleared, and the hot July sun-rays poured down with a scorching intensity. There was a deep, unbroken silence brooding over the entire battle field, like that awful calm of death that rests on an ice-bound sea, and to a casual observer it seemed as if the battle were over. But it was evident to the Federals on the heights—as they waited under the hot mid-day's sun-rays, with throbbing hearts and with preoccupied thoughts too deep for words—that the Confederates were making gigantic preparations for a last desperate and, if possible, crowning effort for victory. The Confederates had massed their artillery on Seminary Hill, and a few minutes before one o'clock the death-like silence was broken by the sharp, ringing report of a Whitworth gun. It was the signal for the battle. Instantly a huge sheet of flame leaped above Seminary Hill, and the thundering roar of a hundred and forty-five cannons filled the air, while their mouths poured death and destruction into the Federal lines. The National commanders ordered their men to lie down on the ground, and to seek every protection possible behind walls, ledges and bowlders. But in spite of every precaution the destruction of life was fearful. Solid shot, shell, canister and grape fell thick amid the Federals with deadly effect. Men and horses were cut to pieces, gun-carriages smashed, caissons with their ammunition exploded, and rocks and trees shattered to fragments. For a quarter of an hour their cannons hurled destruction into the Federal lines, without a reply. Then came the National answer, all along the battle line, from the fiery mouths of three hundred guns, and from Cemetery Hill to Round Top rolled billows of flame, like a sea of fire. The roar of the artillery and the flash of fire was terrific, rivaling in its grandeur the wildest thunder storms of nature. The air was filled with every form of deadly missile, the very earth shook under the combatants' feet, and the rocks and trees waved and moved as if endowed with life, while the men staggered about amid the concussed air, on the trembling earth, as if intoxicated. Thus for two hours thundered this gigantic artillery battle—of over four hundred guns—the greatest the American continent had ever known, and one of the greatest artillery contests of the world; realizing, in its fierce, wild grandeur, one of the most magnificent, soul-stirring and terror-inspiring scenes of earth!

* * * * *

At the end of two hours there came a lull from both sides in the terrific cannonade, and immediately the Confederates began forming in line for a final and desperate charge for victory, the *most bloody and determined of all those four years of war!* As they emerged from the trees that covered the summit of Seminary Hill, and moved steadily and firmly down its slope, with their lines dressed as well as men on parade, it was a magnificent sight, and won even a thrill of admiration from the breasts of those above. They were about a mile distant from the Federal works, and to reach them they had to descend a hill, cross a small valley, and then climb a hill. They numbered about 18,000 men, and were formed in double line of battle, with Pickett's Veteran Virginians leading. As the attacking men moved down the slope, the National troops on the Heights poured a heavy artillery fire upon them; but forward they pressed, with a steady tread and without a waver, though the solid shot and shell were crashing through their ranks at every step. They had advanced about half way when suddenly their cannons, which had been firing over their heads, became silent. "What is the reason?" exclaimed the men, rushing into the vortex of death. "Why?" asked the Confederates gazing on. "Why?" wondered the Federals on the Heights. None knew—not even General Lee—till afterward. The gunners had *exhausted their ammunition!* And there, *unaided*, for half a mile they must breast alone the storm of shot and shell. But on they pressed, with a firm front and steady step, seemingly heedless of every fire and fearless of every foe. The Federals now opened a murderous fire; the bullets fell on the advancing troops like hail on a winter's day, and the cannon balls, shells and canister, ploughed through their ranks, tearing wide gaps in their front; but on they pressed, up the death-swept slope of Cemetery Hill, fearless of the deadly missiles, and heedless of their comrades who were being torn to pieces by their sides. As they advance, it becomes one incessant storm of death-dealing volleys. Along every inch of their front reared the red crest of Destruction! But those true heroes, splashing blood at every step, seemed more eager to court death than to escape danger. As they approached the National line, the ledges and walls literally blazed with a withering fire, until the air along their front grew black with the wings of death. But forward press the Confederates. "Will no fire, no loss, drive them back?" exclaim the Federals.

Before this terrific artillery and musketry fire all the Confederates except Pickett's brave Virginians have melted away—wounded, dead, or driven from the field.

The Federal gunners had now fired away their last round of canister, and, withdrawing their guns, awaited the great struggle between the opposing infantry. The Virginians were now about two hundred yards distant, and for the first time since they had begun to face this terrific storm of death they poured forth well directed volley after volley. The National troops reserved their fire till the enemy was within about eighty yards, then they poured upon them a perfect storm of bullets. So incessant and continuous was the rain of bullets, that it is said that the advancing men turned their heads to one side, like men facing a driving hail storm. But, with a desperate determination, onward rush the brave Virginians. As they near the stone wall they are met by a new danger. The National artillerymen farther up the hill lower the muzzles of their guns, and pour rapid volleys of canister and grape through their ranks; but, heedless of this, they rush rapidly forward, and, vaulting over the breastworks, plant their battle flags on the walls. But they were now confronted by a foe of equal determination and bravery. A veteran division, that had passed through all the bloody battles of the Peninsular campaign; men who had been schooled on the field of death, and who met them with a firm resolution to win or fall. On neither side was there any shrinking, but, on the contrary, both combatants were eager to meet in the desperate struggle!

It was a face-to-face and hand-to-hand contest, fought with a desperation akin to death. So close were the men together, that their clothes were burnt by the exploding cartridges. The Federals, in their eagerness to fall upon the enemy, had lost their regimental organization, but each man was resolute and firm. The struggle now raged fierce and wild. But the end was near. The Virginians pressed on every side, and the Federals in their front, falling upon them with tremendous fury, they were forced back. In an instant the waiting gunners above sprang to their guns, and poured volley after volley through their ranks. At the same time the cannons on their flanks and in their rear opened upon them with terrific effect. The Virginians staggered, reeled, and fell in heaps on the blood-stained field as their ranks were cut to pieces in every direction. They have fought nobly, like true heroes, but they could do no more, and there remained but one course for the few who were left—to retrace their steps across the valley of death! *And thus the curtain fell on the disaster of the master-act of the great Confederate General!*

General Lee had watched with the deepest interest the result of the charge of the brave Virginians, and when he saw it fail he placed his finger on his lips, and for a moment there came over his noble face a shadow of disappointment—that calm, marble-like face that had never been known before, on any battle field of the war, to show either a sign of disappointment or of triumph. In that sad moment he must have felt his disappointment bitterly, for perhaps he may have had a foreboding of that future when the star of the Confederacy should forever set. To an English officer near him, who had come to witness the battle, he said: "This has been a sad day for us, Colonel—a sad day; but we can't always expect to win victories."

But, whatever his thoughts were, the action of the great commander was truly sublime, for, as he rode toward the front through the broken troops, rallying them with such cheering words as: "Never mind, we'll talk of this afterward; now we want all good men to rally," his face was placid and cheerful, showing not a sign of annoyance or dismay. Even for the wounded he had words of kindness, and many of them as they were borne past took off their hats and cheered him. It was a grand, affecting and inspiring scene to see the implicit faith of those troops in their commander as he moved among them, and they formed in regiments, and lay down calmly and quietly in the places assigned them.

Gen. Imboden, one of Lee's staff officers, for whom he had sent, gives us a touching and pathetic picture of the great Confederate commander as he saw him soon after midnight, on the night after the battle. When Imboden reached him he was entirely alone, and had alighted from his horse; and, says that officer, "He threw his arms across his saddle to rest himself, and leaned in silence on his equally weary horse, the two forming a striking group, as motionless as a statue. The bright moon shone full upon his massive features and revealed an expression of sadness I had never seen on that fine face before, in all the vicissitudes of the war through which he had passed. I waited for him to speak, until the silence became painful and embarrassing, when, to break it and change the current of his thoughts, I remarked in a sympathetic tone: 'General, this has been a hard day on you.' This attracted his attention. He looked up and replied mournfully: 'Yes, it has been a sad day for us,' and immediately relapsed into his former mood and attitude."

After a few moments of silence he turned to Imboden, as he raised himself erect, exclaiming excitedly: "General, I never saw troops behave more magnificently than Pickett's division of Virginians did to-day in their grand charge upon the enemy. And if they had been supported as they ought to have been—but for some reason unknown to me they were not—we would have held the position they so gloriously won, and the day would have been ours." Then, in a tone of the deepest sorrow, he added: "Too bad! too bad!! oh, too bad!!!" What terrible agony he felt at that moment no words can depict.

With this desperate charge of Pickett's Virginians, really ended the battle, for although there was another attempt on the Federal lines, it was feeble and of little consequence. The loss of the Virginians in this last charge had been frightful. Their regiments were actually cut to pieces. A ghastly example was where a regiment entered the charge numbering two hundred and fifty and returned with but thirty-eight men.

Thus for three weary days was fought, and thus was won, the great battle of Gettysburg—the most decisive and bloody of all the conflicts of the Civil War. And through that baptism of blood of the magnificent amphitheatre at Gettysburg was turned the fortunes of the Confederacy, for although her soldiers struggled heroically for two years longer, her star gradually waned until it set forever on an April day. Gettysburg was not only great, in being one of the bloody conflicts of the world, but, like Waterloo, it was great in the greatness of its results. Waterloo decreed a change of dynasties, and rang the curtain down forever on a great man's colossal ambition; and Gettysburg was the death of a nation, the restoration of another, and the *shattering of the chains of four million slaves!*

When that last day was done on the battle field, it was literally a baptism of blood, for its rocks were sprayed with blood, its streams and pools were crimsoned, and its wheat fields were beaten into a red mire, while down the few stalks of grain that were standing *trickled tiny globules of blood!*

Night closed over the scene, but ere long a full moon arose and shed a bright light

"O'er the weltering field of tombless dead."

It was a sad and ghastly scene that the moonbeams fell upon; for as thick on the field as leaves in autumn lay the mangled bodies of the slain, while the ground was wet and crimsoned with the blood of 44,567 men who had fallen dead and wounded in that cyclopean contest!

CHAPTER XI.

THE STRUGGLE WITH DEATH.

"INTO a ward of the whitewashed halls,
 Where the dead and dying lay,
Wounded by bayonets, shells and balls,
Somebody's darling was borne one day.
Somebody wept when he marched away,
 Looking so handsome, brave and grand;
Somebody's kiss on his forehead lay,
 And some one clung to his parting hand."

AT the open upper window of a house overlooking, and even above the field of strife, a girl's beautiful, curly head was leaning on a little dimpled hand, while her arm rested on the window-sill. Her large, lustrous eyes were eagerly watching the terrible struggle about Little Round Top, and as she rested there it would have required but a single glance of those who knew her to have recognized in the girl's finely formed bust—as full and gracefully rounded as a sculptor's model—the demi-figure of Bertha Merton. Her face was very pale, but very beautiful, for there was a deep, intellectual interest expressed on it, and a tender sweetness in the large, liquid eyes, as they drank in a prominent figure, leading amid the thickest of the fight—that of General Charles Landon. For he had been promoted to the command of a brigade, a short time before, for gallantry on the field.

It was the second day of the Battle of Gettysburg. General Longstreet's men were making their terrific charge on the Federal position, and the long lines of men in gray had lapped about Little Round Top—that steep, rocky eminence that towered above the rest—the key of the battle field, which the Confederates wished to win, and which the Federals were determined not to lose.

Around the rocky height, the battle raged wild and furious, the artillery on its summit poured forth a murderous fire, while behind every ledge and boulder flashed forth the blaze of musketry. Into this vortex of fire, smoke and death charged the shadowy lines of men in gray, as if endeavoring to choke the volcano with human bodies. But the Federals met every advance of the serried ranks with a heavy fire and a wall of gleaming steel. Amid the blue lines, where the conflict raged the hottest, rode Charlie Landon. Upon his pale face there was a calm, determined expression, for his lips were set, and there was a daring glitter in his dark eyes that showed his brave, resolute nature.

Bertha raised the spy glass she held in her hand and swept the field until its focus rested on Charlie Landon's superb figure, conspicuous amid the storm of battle by its graceful, commanding appearance. And no wonder the sight aroused a thrill of admiration in her breast, for his noble bearing, and his fine form and head, clearly outlined against the fire and smoke, would have won respect even from a foe.

As she was eagerly watching him he suddenly turned his horse so as to almost face her—his coat was wide open, for the heat was intense—when to her dismay she saw that his white shirt front was half *crimson with his blood.*

She lowered the spy glass, and there came a wild, frightened look into the large, dark eyes, that told of anticipated tragedy. In a moment she raised the small telescope, and gazed eagerly at his figure, like one under the spell of some weird fascination, while in the velvety depths of her eyes there remained that haunted look of expected calamity. As she watched his conspicuous figure amid the battle she saw him reel in the saddle, *and fall!*

The tragedy she had anticipated had come, and as she dropped the glass her eyes filled with tears, and the little head fell heavily on her arms, as in her sorrow she realized how dearly she loved him still.

In a few moments she raised her head, and, brushing away the tears that were trickling down her cheeks, sprang quickly to her feet, as she muttered to herself: "This will not do. I must not give way to grief, when perhaps I might be of assistance to him."

Catching up a buffalo robe that lay on a chair, she threw it over her arm, and hastened from the house. She walked rapidly forward, and each moment, as she drew nearer and nearer the battle, she met the soldiers bringing away the wounded, until those bearing new sufferers became one continuous stream. And then the roar of the conflict became almost deafening, while the bullets fell thick about her; but heedless and fearless of them, she hurried onward. At last she saw *his* well known form lying on a litter, borne by two soldiers; although he was insensible, he still breathed strong and regularly. She sprang to the side of the litter, which was a rude wooden affair, without any padding, or even a covering of cloth.

"Oh!" she exclaimed, as she stood by the litter, "don't those rough slats hurt him?"

"Yes," replied one of the men, "they seemed to hurt him severely, for, although he is insensible, he groaned several times as we carried him along. But it was the best we could do."

"But can't we put this buffalo robe under him?" she asked, taking it from her arm.

"Yes, that is the very thing. It is fortunate that you brought it."

They gently raised him, while Bertha's nimble little hands soon placed the robe beneath; and as his bruised body sank on the soft bed, she heard, or imagined she heard, a sigh of relief issue from his lips. As he lay there, so pale and handsome, on the white robe—as yet but slightly stained with his blood—she, in spite of her sorrow and deep concern, became irresistibly entranced by the statuesque beauty—yet thrilled with life—of his fine face and form. In her artistic nature, she seemed to realize in the beautiful form before her, how the Greek heroes of old—whom Homer loved to picture—must have appeared as they lay on the battle field before Troy. Those wondrous pictures Homer gives us in the Iliad, of the flower of the youth of Greece and Troy, lying on the field of battle "in the stately repose of death," their blood enriching in color, by its crimson contrast, their marble white temples and blood-stained curls of gold. So sublimely beautiful does Homer paint the ancient youth with their war-stained curls, in the serene, pathetic beauty of death, like some exquisite statue, about which the color of life still lingers, that he fascinates us, and almost wins us to love wounds and death. And as Charlie lay there among the soft folds of the white robe, with the form of a Greek hero and the head of an Apollo, the red blood staining like a wreath of carnation the dark curls that clustered about his white brow, while so serene was the expression of his face, so fine and beautiful the blending of the crimson with the dark hair, in the battle-stained curls, that it brought no suggestion of horror or distaste to her artistic nature, as she thought, so must have appeared the greatest of the old Greek heroes, Achilles, as he lay before the Scæan gate of Troy.

She was roused from her reverie by one of the soldiers remarking: "That robe is the very thing. He rests easily upon it. Which way shall we carry him?"

"To the house yonder," she replied, bursting into tears.

They carried him to the house, and up into the room she had left but a short time before, and laid him on the bed. Then the men departed, but one of them soon returned, accompanied by a surgeon. Although the surgeon was young in years, he soon showed that he lacked neither skill nor experience, for he quickly extracted the bullet from the wounded man's arm, and ligated the severed artery, from which the blood was flowing. He then turned his attention to the wound in Landon's breast. The bullet had penetrated painfully near the heart, and as Bertha assisted him to dress the wound he replied, in answer to her eager question, "It's a very dangerous wound, and he is very weak from the loss of blood. He must have remained for some time in the saddle after being struck by the bullets, and all the while the wounds were bleeding. But while there's life there's hope. But it will be several days before he regains consciousness."

After he had applied a styptic to the wound and dressed it, he said: "Here is a prescription; get it filled, and give him some of the medicine as soon as you can get him to swallow. I suppose the General is your brother?" he continued.

He did not notice the blush that suffused her tear-stained cheeks, for he was gazing down at the wounded soldier; and without waiting for an answer he continued, as an excuse for his hurry: "I must leave him now. In all the battles of the war in which I have been engaged, I have never seen so many wounded men before. The surgeons are nearly worn out. But my little lady," he added, kindly, as he saw fresh tears fill her eyes, "keep up a brave heart, and you may win him back to health again. I will return to assist you all in my power at the earliest opportunity."

When the surgeon had departed, her overstrung nerves could bear the tension no longer, and, leaning her head upon her arms, she burst into a flood of tears. And as she sobbed, she felt the old love for him came back with treble its former force, as she remembered the happy bygone days they had spent together. "And oh!" she thought, "if he should die, it would be the end—the dreadful end of all my happy dreams!" After weeping she felt better, for her trials and sorrows seemed to become dispersed on the bright wings of Hope. For physiologists tell us that tears are nature's remedies, which relieve and soothe the nervous system from overpowering griefs and burdens. After bathing her face, she went to a hospital and obtained the medicine. On her return she occupied herself for some time in making the poor fellow as comfortable as possible, with that tender care that a woman intuitively knows so well how to do. Then she sat down in a chair by a window, as she felt unreservedly that it was her duty to nurse and protect him during his helplessness. Her pride and waywardness had fled; she thought only of doing all in her power for him, as she prayed that God might give her strength to nurse him back to health; and unhesitatingly would she have risked her life to save his.

What a mystery and seeming contradiction, yet wondrous power is woman. Place her in a conservatory, foster and indulge her every whim, and she becomes a thing of fancy, waywardness and frivolity—annoyed by a dewdrop, fretted by a thorn, ready to faint at the sight of a beetle or a mouse, and starting back affrighted at the darkness. But let a dire calamity come, arouse her sympathy and affection, enkindle the fires of her heart, and then behold the wonderful change! What a wealth of affection and strength is in her heart! Transplant her in a new field, give her a weakly animal or a child to protect, or, on the field of battle, a wounded soldier to attend and care for; see her then lift her own white arms as a shield, heedless of her once crimson cheeks, that are growing pale as she wears her life away to aid the helpless. Watch her in the dark places of earth, as she disputes, step by step, the march of disease, pestilence and death, while others, seemingly stronger and braver, shrink away. Silently, calmly, nobly she meets misfortune, faces pain and danger—with less timidity than she formerly met an admiring gaze—and ever with consolation in her heart, and a blessing on her lips. In the hour of triumph and splendor, she appears a butterfly of uselessness, but let adversity come, then behold her true worth—a diamond of the first water, freed from the dross! Thus woman is a wondrous mystery, from whom radiates the charm of the darkest places, as well as the brightest spots of earth!

As Bertha sat there in the afternoon's waning light, she could not help watching his handsome face with admiration. And lying there, he really formed a fine picture of manly beauty, his face slightly turned to one side, and his head reclining lightly on his arm, which was half buried in the snowy pillow; his dark hair curling in a profusion of ringlets over his pale brow, his cheeks plump and white—where not browned by exposure; his dark brown moustache shading the mouth and dimpled chin with the old, familiar boyish sweetness about them she remembered so well; the collar of his shirt was rolled back, exposing the white, round throat, which arose gracefully from the firm, square shoulders, almost as plump as those of a girl; his eyes were gently closed, hiding the light in them, which she had seen so often melt into softness in the presence of those he loved, or glitter with daring when facing a foe; he breathed lightly, and seemed to be resting easily, except for an occasional twinge of the muscles of the neck and shoulder, which showed that he suffered pain. Altogether, viewed in the afternoon's sunlight, it was a face few could look upon and not admire and trust. And there came into her heart an irresistible longing to possess a picture of that noble face she loved so dearly, for she felt it would lighten her sorrow to still retain the image of his face, although he should be taken from her forever. She brought the best sketching material she could find, and went quietly and eagerly to work, and although she had done no artistic work since leaving St. Arlyle, she found she was as skillful as ever with the pencil and brush. Seated by a small table in the waning light of that sultry July afternoon, with the battle raging so near that the smoke and roar of the cannon rolled into the room, while the concussion of the great guns shook the house, she applied herself diligently in making a drawing of the face she cherished so dearly and feared she might lose forever.

As she drew the outlines of his face, all the old love welled up in her heart, and as she gazed with inexpressible pity and emotion upon him, there came over her a sudden irresistible impulse, and, walking to the bed, she knelt by his side and dropped a kiss upon his lips, as silently and lightly as a dew-drop falls, as she murmured: "Oh! my poor boy! My poor boy!"

She drew back, almost affrighted, as her face grew crimson and hot with shame, for she thought she saw his eyes partly open and his lips move. But this must have been a momentary delusion, caused by her agitation, for when she looked again he still lay in the same unconscious state.

Thus during the afternoon, when not attending to the wounded soldier, she occupied herself at her drawing. Night came, and with it the close of the second day of the battle, and her portrait was nearly finished.

It was almost noon the next day before she was able to resume her drawing. The last sounds of the conflict had died away early in the morning, and the warm sultry air swept into the room amid a deep silence, only broken by the noise of her brush or pencil on the canvas. But it was the calm soon to be broken by that memorable storm of destruction of the 3d of July, that through all the after years of her life she never could forget.

The little clock on the shelf had almost marked the hour of one, when there came a terrific roar from the Confederate guns that shook the house. For nearly fifteen minutes they roared away without a reply. Then came the Federal answer, all alone their line, from the mouths of almost 300 cannon. The roar of the artillery was fearful; the house shook and rocked till it seemed to her like a ship in a gale; the window panes were shattered to fragments and the glass strewn on the floor; the table before her seemed to dance, while her hand seemed to beat about on the canvas. She could not remain quiet, but rushed repeatedly to the window and gazed out; she could see nothing but the thick clouds of sulphurous smoke, amid which flashed the flames from the cannons' mouths. From the window she repeatedly went to the wounded soldier's side and gazed at his face, but he always lay in the same trance-like sleep—unconscious of it all. Thus for two hours raged the terrible storm of human wrath; then came a lull in the mighty cannonade. Then she watched eagerly and excitedly the last desperate struggle for victory between the opposing infantry, as Pickett's Virginians charged fiercely and stubbornly up the hill amid the storm of bullets and balls, while the smoke hung about their partly hidden ranks, like banks of mist. Thus the afternoon wore away, and the sun sank lower and lower, till it appeared a great fiery ball in the west; then she saw the Confederates fall back in wild confusion, and she knew their charge had failed, and that the great battle of Gettysburg was ended!

She sat in silence by the window till the last beams of day faded, and the flashes and reports of the pickets' muskets grew less and less frequent, till at last they became silent in the gathering gloom; then, as the sentinel stars began to fill the sky, there came into her heart a feeling of sadness —a feeling of impending grief and pain, hanging over her like a black pall! Can it be possible that in the hidden and mysterious workings of the mind, there came to her a premonition of the loss and sorrow the darkness was bringing? For that night, on the battle field, she lost forever, by a picket's random shot, one of the dearest and truest friends of her girlhood, although she did not learn of it until long afterward.

Throughout the mighty roar of the battle, and for weeks after, Charlie Landon remained unconscious. For consciousness had entirely left him from the moment he fell from his horse, while resisting at the head of his men the fierce charge of the Confederate infantry. He felt the sharp sting of the bullet wounds in his arm and breast, but, heedless of them, he rode onward, until from the loss of blood he grew suddenly faint, and there seemed to dart through his brain a thousand flashes of light, mingled with a terrible roar, while the sun grew suddenly dark, and he seemed to be falling into an immense black gulf; and then consciousness left him. The first faint revival of feeling was followed by a succession of dreams of the wildest imaginable sufferings. He was crushed beneath the wheels of the wheels of the Juggernaut car. He was stretched on the bed of Procrustes, while the inhuman Damaster hacked and pulled his limbs asunder. He was Tantalus, in water up to his chin, yet unable to quench his burning thirst. He was Tityus, chained to a rock, while the vultures were constantly gnawing at his vitals. Then came a delightful change in his visions. An angelic face hovered above him, while soft, gentle hands cooled his parched lips and bathed his burning brow. And oh! how sweet and delicious it all was! Then the old horrors would return, but ere long the same sweet, sympathetic face would float above him, and the same gentle hands, with ice cold water, would quench his burning thirst and cool his aching brow. Once he thought the beautiful face bent down and kissed him tenderly. And then he thought how much its features resembled Bertha's lovely face.

At last, one day toward the close of August, he awoke perfectly rational. It was an exquisite summer afternoon, and the balmy air swept into the room, laden with the redolence of tree and flower, and he lay in the large, cool, airy apartment with a delicious feeling of pleasure and rest. As he turned his head on the pillow he made a slight noise. Instantly a girlish figure reading near the window glanced toward the bed, and then glided from the room. But not before he had recognized the beautiful face of Bertha, the same sweet, pitying face that he had seen in all his dreams.

From that day his recovery was rapid. But he did not see again the face he most wished to look upon with the deepest yearnings of his heart. And his first inquiry, when he was able to be about the room, was for her. They informed him that she had sailed from New York for Rome, there to study painting for the next two years. It was a bitter disappointment to him, but he bore it bravely. The first day he was able to walk about the room, he found lying on the table a dainty blue gold-banded cap that he had often seen Bertha wear. It had been presented to her by the wounded soldiers of a Fredericksburg hospital, during their convalescence, as a tribute of their gratitude for her many deeds of kindness to them. He took up the cap almost reverentially, and placed it in the breast pocket of his coat, as he thought it was the last memento of the girl he still truly and tenderly loved, and who in his helplessness had with her own hands guarded him from death. And he felt how readily, yea, gladly, would he give the life she had saved to prove his gratitude and love for her. "But alas!" he thought sadly, "we may never meet again, but I shall love her truly as long as life remains. May Heaven protect her, and shower its brightest blessings on her curly head!"

When he had gained sufficient strength he joined his brigade again, and followed the fortunes of the Army of the Potomac to the close of the war.

CHAPTER XII.

AT REST IN HEAVEN.

Virtus requiei nescia sordidæ.

FOR none return from those quiet shores
Who cross with the boatman cold and pale;
We hear the dip of the golden oars,
And catch a gleam of the snowy sail;
And lo! they have passed from our yearning hearts.
—*N. A. Priest.*

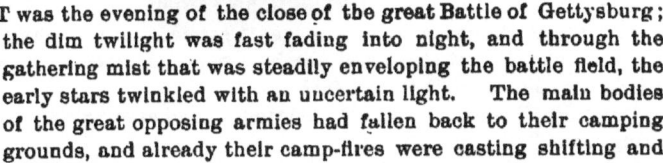

IT was the evening of the close of the great Battle of Gettysburg; the dim twilight was fast fading into night, and through the gathering mist that was steadily enveloping the battle field, the early stars twinkled with an uncertain light. The main bodies of the great opposing armies had fallen back to their camping grounds, and already their camp-fires were casting shifting and fantastic flashes of light and shadow on the banks of mist and the adjoining trees. The advanced pickets of the contending forces—who were not more than three-quarters of a mile apart—kept up a desultory fire at each other, as the red flashes darting through the mist, followed by the whiz of bullets, plainly told.

Colonel Edward Wilberton was riding along the Confederate picket line, when in the gathering gloom he suddenly thought he saw a familiar figure near him, and, turning his horse, he rode toward it. He was not mistaken, for it was his wife, May, who had just arisen from dressing a soldier's wound and giving him a drink of spirits. As her husband approached her he cried excitedly, as he heard a bullet hum past his head:

"May, for Heaven's sake go back! This is no place for you. You are recklessly risking your life!"

"But what will become of this wounded man?" asked the noble girl.

"I will send an ambulance to remove him," he answered, as he sprang from his horse. And as hurried toward her, he exclaimed excitedly: "Hurry, May! You must not stay here! I will go with you, but for my sake be quick! It is dangerous, my darling!"

The words had scarcely left his lips, when she was struck full in the left breast by a bullet. But before she fell he caught her in his arms, as he cried: "Oh my darling!"

He pillowed her head on his breast, just as the warm blood spurted over her dress, staining it a crimson hue. He hastily tore open the bosom of her dress, and endeavored to staunch the flow with his handkerchief, but in vain. It poured forth, deluging the snowy breasts and crimsoning the golden hair, that had fallen over her shoulders.

"Oh my darling! you are dying!" he cried in agony.

"Don't feel so bad, Edward dear, cried the noble girl. "I'm in God's hands and ——"

Her head fell against his shoulder, and the words died on her lips. He placed his canteen to her lips, and after a few sips she rallied, and throwing her arm around his neck, rested calmly in his encircling arms. For often, on the battle field, the wound that is mortal is painless, and so hers seemed to be, for after a moment she raised her blue eyes, and looking into his face with all a woman's tender trust, said:

"Don't cry, Edward. I'm not suffering. And above all are God's everlasting arms."

After a moment's silence she continued: "I want you to tell Bertha when you see her, that my last moments were peaceful and happy. And tell her to crush back her pride and to be true to her own heart's love, and Heaven will bless her."

She grew rapidly weaker, as she said, with a struggle: "Good bye, my boy. Don't feel so bad. We've had a happy life together. It seems hard to go. Yet God's will be done. I shall surely meet you on the shining shore of peace. Farewell!"

"Oh, my darling May," he cried, as her arm tightened convulsively and passionately around his neck, and her eyes eagerly sought his, with a last, wild, loving glance. Then the little hand relaxed its grasp on his neck, and the snowy eyelids drooped forever over the sweet blue eyes. He bent his head quickly and kissed the red lips, as with her parting breath a heavenly smile flitted over them, then as his head sank on her breast, he felt the last throb of her heart, and he knew that her rosy lips would never smile upon him again, and that her sweet blue eyes would never greet him more!

The mist had melted away, and the last rays of twilight fell full upon her dainty, drooping form, yet beautiful, even in death, and seemingly clinging to him, just as she had clung with her last parting strength; while he still clasped her form with all the tenderness of his deep love! Thus solemnly the last light faded and night enveloped the Pennsylvania hills—and dark and gloomy it fell upon him. In that long, sorrowful night that closed around him, sprang forth the shadowy spectres of sweet memories, hopes and affections that haunted him but to remind him that they were dead; yet at first he did not fully realize his loss. It came upon him by degrees, with a feeling of desolation—like one alone on a rocky isle—that his first love, and that his brightest hopes, dreams and wishes were shattered forever! The night wore on, and the full moon shed its light over the field, but still he remained, grasping the beloved form, motionless, dazed and bewildered, like one in a dream. The clear silvery moonlight fell full upon her form, where yet lingered the wondrous beauty of her slender, rounded figure, with the long, light colored hair, the beautiful white face, as finely moulded as that of a statue, the snowy eyelids fringed by the long dark lashes, the fine cut lips, as tenderly wreathed in a smile as if yet animated with life, the throat and shoulders round and white, and the snowy breasts beautifully carved and unmarred in their whiteness, except for the small red wound, which showed where the tide of life had ebbed away. Thus unchanged,

"Death lay on her like an untimely frost
Upon the sweetest flower of all the field."

Long after midnight they found him, still clinging to her dead form. They bore her body into camp, and he followed, like one in a trance. The next day he had her body sent away to be buried in the St. Arlyle graveyard. Then with a broken and bruised heart he joined his regiment again, and fought through the war to the bitter end. No wonder those few Southern soldiers remaining toward the close of the war resisted so stubbornly and desperately though they knew their cause was hopeless, for by the loss of their homes, firesides, and—like Edward Wilberton—those they had loved as dearly as their own lives, they grew fearless and reckless, till even death itself had no terrors for them!

CHAPTER XIII.

NEARING THE END.

"NIGHT closed around the conqueror's way,
  And lightning showed the distant hills,
Where those who lost that dreadful day
Stood few and faint, but fearless still."

WE now come to the closing scenes of the Civil War. The days of the last conflicts around Richmond, on old Virginia's blood-stained soil. General Grant's immense army had been pouring, day and night, for weeks, a heavy fire with mortar, cannon and musket upon the Confederate lines in front of Petersburg. When a Federal fell he was replaced by a recruit. But when a Confederate was killed his place remained vacant. Death, disease and desertion had so reduced Lee's army in those last days in March, 1865, that he did not have one man to every ten feet of fortification. Starvation stared them in the face, like a hungry wolf, for unbolted corn and black molasses were their only rations, and even these were dealt out to them in meager quantities, while their clothing was in rags, and hundreds of them were almost barefooted. Grant's great army gave them no rest, and men who fought all day to save one point were marched all night to be ready to save another. Tired and worn out, the Confederate soldiers fell asleep but to be awakened by the bursting of shells in their midst, or by the fierce attack of their assailants. During their last long defense of Petersburg and Richmond, when it must have been as apparent to all that their cause was hopeless as it was to Lee himself, they struggled on through a sea of troubles and hardships with a patriotism and devotion that the world must ever acknowledge was truly heroic.

Meanwhile, every day Grant's great army was extending its lines and encircling them like an immense boa constrictor. And in the grimness of despair the Confederate chieftain resolved to make a daring and desperate effort to pierce the mighty Federal army that was crushing him in its folds.

This daring venture was an attempt to penetrate and cut the mighty Federal army through its center. The plan was to attack Fort Steadman (one of Grant's strongest and most advanced forts) at night, and also the three other forts commanding it; then, after capturing them, to push forward and fall upon the rear of the National army. By thus surprising the great army at night it would give the Confederates a chance of success. And if the forts were captured the Federal army would be cut in two, and thrown into confusion.

A few minutes before midnight, on the 25th of March, the Confederates silently assembled at their salient point, in front of the fort, to be ready to rush upon it. Every man was prepared and knew the work before him. The open space over which they must rush could be swept by over thirty Federal cannon and more than five thousand muskets. Every detail had been planned, and the last preparation was for each Confederate to tie a white cloth around his arm, so that he could be recognized by his comrades in the dark.

First rushed across the open space about two hundred men, armed with axes, who in five minutes cut down the abatis in front of the fort. Had these men attempted to cross the space by daylight not one of them would have lived two minutes. Following these men came the storming columns of infantry, who, after capturing the pickets, swarmed into the fort. So surprised were the Federals in the fort that they offered no resistance, for when they sprang to their feet they were confronted by Confederate bayonets. After capturing the fort the attacking columns pressed forward, but in the darkness the guides became confused, and the men were unable to find the works that commanded Fort Steadman, and with breaking of day the Confederates were compelled to retreat to the captured works, and General Gordon, who had directed the assault, made preparations to hold the fort.

The moment daylight broke the Federal artillerymen sighted their guns on the fort, while at the same time the Confederates trained their heavy guns to reply, and for over an hour a terrific artillery contest was maintained. Round shot, shell and grape fell so rapidly into the fort that soon every gun in it was silenced, and the ground inside was covered with dead and wounded. But still the Confederates clung to the fort, and although the Federals made three charges upon it, they were received with such a heavy musketry fire that they were compelled to fall back. But gradually the mighty Federal army drew closer and closer, and finally an entire corps prepared to assault the fort. There now only remained for the Confederates in the fort either to await capture or to retreat across the narrow open space, swept by the National artillery and musketry.

Hundreds of Confederates attempted to escape by rushing across the open space to their own lines. They started singly, and in numbers, but however they started the result was the same; they were mowed down by the storm of bullets. Men who started alone would be struck by a dozen bullets. And out of squads of thirty or forty who started to cross the vale of death, but two or three would escape. Thus for over an hour they endeavored to escape, till the open space was literally covered with the dead. These retreats gradually weakened the force in the fort, and it was finally carried by a Federal charge.

General Lee had staked all in this last desperate venture and lost, and that night his force was weaker by fifteen hundred men. The cloud that had ever hung over the stormy events of the Confederacy, often growing bright in the early days of the war, but to suddenly grow dark at Gettysburg, and again on the battle field of the Wilderness, had now grown blacker and more threatening, till its heavy shadow told unmistakably of the impending end!

* * * * *

In this battle fell several of St. Arlyle's men, and among them Bertha lost, that night, one of the truest and best friends of her girlhood, noble Dr. Granville. In exposing himself, with his accustomed bravery, wherever the cause of suffering humanity led, he sprang conspicuously on one of the redoubts to rescue a wounded soldier. A perfect storm of bullets fell around him; and it was the last time many of the men ever saw his stately and well known form, for he was struck full in the breast by a bullet from a sharpshooter's rifle, and fell mortally wounded into the arms of an officer of the St. Arlyle regiment, who with the assistance of others bore him to the rear.

They soon found a surgeon, who, after dressing the wound, recognized in his patient a former friend, whom he had not seen for years. As their eyes met the former exclaimed:

"Why, it is Benjamin Granville! Do you remember me?"

"Yes, very well," replied Dr. Granville.

"I once did you a great injury, long years ago, and I have been sorry for it many times since. Can you forgive me?" said the surgeon.

"Yes," replied Dr. Granville, "for I forgave you many years ago. You know Bacon says, 'He that cannot forgive others, breaks down the bridge over which he must pass himself.' And one of the noblest lessons I've learned in life is to forgive, and, as far as the heart can, to forget, so that through the march of years my heart has grown lighter and more peaceful as I descend life's rugged pathway. Thus it becomes the calmest and happiest, just before the tomb, like a flower of spring time, the brightest before it fades."

"What do you think of my case?" Dr. Granville asked suddenly.

"It is a very dangerous wound," replied the old surgeon, as he shook his head sadly.

"Yes, as a surgeon, I understand it full well," said Dr. Granville. "The wound is mortal. I had hoped to live to see peace again. But I submit to a higher will than mine. It was my greatest wish to see my country again at peace. For I think the Republic's grandest glory is just beginning to dawn through the vista of coming years. For the brightest years and noblest are often those after emerging from the gloom of strife and care, like the bright sunshine that bursts at last through a stormy sky, flooding all around. And I still believe a republic is the true form of government, for it is based on the principles of equal rights to all, equal on earth, as they will be in Heaven, rewarded when they do right, punished when they do wrong."

At that moment one of Dr. Granville's friends approached his bed and said:

"Oh, I am so sorry your case is hopeless!"

"No, not hopeless," said the noble man, "for I still have Heaven. And there is nothing so sweet in life as going home to Heaven. Tired with the struggles of earth, we lay down the burden at last, for the eternal rest. For God has said, 'Be thou faithful unto death and I will give thee a crown of life.'"

He lingered on in pain until evening, but no word of complaint or moan escaped his lips, lest those around him in the hospital tent, less dangerously wounded than himself, should hear it and feel discouraged. As the darkness closed around and the "cease firing" was sounded through the Federal lines, a smile stole over his face, and those who were beside his bed knelt down to catch his dying words. They were of the happy, peaceful years passed in the little village of St. Arlyle, and in his thoughts he was again in the college class room, once more instructing the students, now scattered over the wide world, for, stretching forth his hand, he said: "It grows dark, students, you may go! But the glorious light is bursting on the other shore!" Then he turned his head wearily on the pillow, and the "light of immortal beauty silently covered his face," as Benjamin Granville yielded up his noble and loving soul to the God who gave it. His grave is in the little church yard in St. Arlyle, and over it stands a marble monument, but his greatest tomb is in the hearts of the men and women who loved him too truly ever to need a marble shaft to remind them of the noble, generous man!

Bertha read of his death in Rome, in an article in an American journal, entitled "A Great Loss to Science." And tears filled her eyes as she realized that in his death she had lost another of the truest and noblest friends of her girlhood's years. And as she sat in the waning light by the window overlooking the waters of the Tiber there arose through the mist of her tears a sea of familiar faces, all victims of the terrible Civil War, and each intimately linked with her own life, some cherished, others dearly beloved. One of them was that of a dark-haired boy, who fell in the early days of the war, on the picket line along the Potomac River, with a bullet through his brave young Irish heart. She remembered well, when they bore him into camp, with the night dew still fresh on his young, pale face, and buried him in a soldier's grave, with a wreath on his breast—a tribute from her own hands.

And another—a man's face, who received his mortal wound on the battle field of Chancellorsville; one who had been wild and wayward, and at times even wicked, but who, ere his heart was stilled forever, had found the perfect faith and peace.

And still another—a sweet, girlish face, with bright blue eyes and sunny hair, who died with a bullet through her pure young heart, on the field of Gettysburg. "Ah my darling May," Bertha murmured, "how little did I think when we wandered together through the shady lanes and over the green meadows of St. Arlyle, and past the little church yard, that you would meet your death on the field of battle, and that your final resting place would so soon be there. Sweet, calm and pale your face must have appeared when you met the end, with kind thoughts and wishes for others, even in the throes of death, like that noble man's face, peaceful and calm, for he feared not death. So will your faces appear on the shore of the great Hereafter, if I am permitted to see them there, only far nobler yet, with the halo of immortal beauty around your heads!"

CHAPTER XIV.

THE DAWN OF PEACE.

BEAUTEOUS peace!
Sweet union of a state! what else but thou
Gives safety, strength, and glory to a people?
—*Thompson.*

N all human events, at some period the curtain falls, and the play is over; so we now come to the last act in the bloody drama of the great Civil War. Even the Confederates knew the end was coming fast. For the shadows were already gathering darkly that were soon to envelop the last faint ray of hope! The shattered Army of Northern Virginia, now reduced to less than eight thousand men, had fallen back to the little town of Appomattox. The Confederate troops were almost in a hopeless condition, their strong works in front of Fredericksburg captured, their lines of retreat and communication severed by their being driven upon the peninsula formed by the James and Appomattox rivers, while in their front the great Federal army was closing upon them in the form of a mighty semicircle, yet, in the grimness of despair, that fragment of the once proud Army of Northern Virginia, like a dying lion at bay, still now and then makes the foe feel the sharp sting of its claws, and still tosses its royal head in defiance.

It was scarcely daylight on the morning of the 9th of April—the day that is to decide the fate of Lee's army—but already the roar of the cannon announces that the battle has begun. As the sun mounts higher the roar of the guns grows louder, and the battle becomes more and more general. And as the serried ranks of the great semicircle approach the Confederates, they catch in the distance, through the trees and underbrush, an occasional glimpse of Sheridan's cavalrymen as they close upon the foe! But the Confederates attack the cavalry savagely, and as they drive it back, a cheer bursts from their ranks, but in a few minutes more their exultation is changed to despair, for they see that the cavalry is but falling back upon the heavy masses of infantry and artillery that form the mighty semicircle that is advancing to envelop them like the irresistible hand of Fate! Rapidly the Federal troops dash over swamp and stream, with the wildest excitement, for they know that unless the enemy can break through their lines within fifteen minutes all is over with the Army of Northern Virginia. As the great semicircle closes about the Confederates, the battle rages all along the line, while the sky becomes ablaze with flame, as the cannons and mortars hurl forth their shot and shell!

Suddenly two horsemen gallop out from the Confederate line, and one of them waves a flag of truce, while the other—heedless of the storm of bullets and balls—rides rapidly across the open space, and, as he gracefully salutes the Federal commander, he says:

"Sir, General Longstreet desires a cessation of hostilities until he can hear from General Lee, as to a proposal of surrender."

Immediately the fire slackens on both sides, and in a few moments more the order is sounded along the Federal line to "cease firing" and to halt. *The die is cast! The end has come!*

A truce is agreed upon until four o'clock in the afternoon. Four o'clock comes, but no word is heard from either of the great commanders, and there is no alternative left but to renew the battle, as the order is issued along the Federal lines: " Prepare to make or receive an attack in ten minutes." The ten minutes elapse, and the Federal skirmishers are pressing forward, when suddenly comes the order to halt, and with it the information that *Lee has surrendered.* Instantly the Federal lines are broken, and cheer after cheer rends the air until late in the night.

Early in the afternoon of that day—the 9th of April, 1865—an officer, accompanied by but a single aid, rode out of the Confederate camp toward the Federal lines. He was mounted on a powerful gray horse, and wore a spotless gray uniform, that fitted his large and finely moulded figure to perfection, while on the collar of his coat glittered the stars of the highest rank of the Confederate Army. There was a natural dignity and modest reserve, blended with a singular, calm gentleness about his every action that would win from the most casual observer respect, even admiration. His hair was as white as the driven snow, his face was very pale, and there was a deep expression of sadness upon it, yet blended with a rare charm of sweetness and intelligence; his brow, thoughtful and grave, was tinged with the shadows of care and sorrow, while his bright eyes lighted up his face with a singular fascination one could not soon forget; but that which would have most attracted one's attention was the calm expression of power and determination, so indelibly imprinted there that it seemed nothing in life could shake. Altogether it was an intellectual face of a man of rare, magnetic, commanding power and penetrating judgment.

As he approached a Confederate outpost, the soldiers saluted, and the officer bowed with a cold smile that rendered his face even more sad. When he had passed, one of the soldiers exclaimed: "It is General Lee, going to surrender the army!"

"Yes," replied another, "and I tell you it's a hard duty for him to perform."

On reaching the house where the terms of surrender were to be arranged, General Lee and his aid, Colonel Marshall, dismounted and entered a small room in the left corner. It was an old styled, double house, with a piazza extending across the front, and was known as the McLean house. In the small room where the interview took place were gathered several officers, and among them were two young men seated at a table, reducing to writing the terms of the surrender of the Army of Northern Virginia to the Army of the Potomac. One of the young men, Colonel Marshall—a great-grandson of Chief Justice Marshall—was acting on behalf of General Lee; the other, a man with a dusky countenance—a grand-nephew of the celebrated Indian chief, Red Jacket—was acting under Ulysses S. Grant.

At a short distance apart, and facing each other, sat two remarkable men; remarkable for having been the chief actors in the great Civil War. The larger and elder of the two was the more impressive in his appearance. His face pale and massive—seemingly with an expression of calm indifference upon it—was surrounded by a mass of snow white hair. There was not a spot upon his bright gray uniform, and the gauntlets which he wore were as white and unsullied as a lady's glove. He was fully equipped with sword, belt and sash. That was General R. E. Lee. The other was a smaller man, with a remarkably determined face, but on which there was now a peculiar expression, like that on a man's countenance who is endeavoring not to give pain, but seems at a loss how to avoid it. In his dress he contrasted strongly with Lee; his boots were almost covered with mud, his uniform, the coat of which was minus several buttons, was splashed with spots of earth, and he wore no sword, belt or sash. All together, he looked like a soldier who had just returned from a rough campaign. That was Ulysses S. Grant, the victor.

The greeting between the two commanders, though short, was courteous, even kind, and they immediately proceeded to business. It was a great and thrilling occasion, and wonderful memories must have crowded upon those two men as they sat face to face. Memories that must have thrilled their hearts as their thoughts wandered back to those stirring scenes during those four years of Civil War, when brothers' swords were wet with brothers' blood, and in which they had been the leading actors on the opposing sides. And now at last the end had come, and they had met together to sheath their swords in peace and drop the curtain forever on one of the most remarkable and bloody dramas of the Nineteenth Century!

In that little room there fell a death-like silence, broken only by the scratch of the secretaries' pens upon the paper, for all felt the overpowering influence of the great scene they were witnessing. The silence was so deep and continuous that at last it became embarrassing, and, to break the spell, General Grant said, apologetically, as he noticed the fully equipped and faultless appearance of Lee, contrasting vividly with his own negligent dress and absence of arms:

"General Lee, I have no sword; I have been riding all night. I do not always carry a sword, because a sword is sometimes a very inconvenient thing."

Lee made no reply, but in a formal, almost haughty manner, bowed with a grace and pride that after all became him so well. Again the silence fell, seemingly deeper and more embarrassing than before. When again, to relieve the awkwardness of the occasion, General Grant asked:

"General Lee, what became of the white horse you rode in Mexico? He might not be dead yet; he was not so old."

Lee bowed in the same formal manner, as he replied:

"I left him at the White house, on the Pamunky river, and I have not seen him since."

At last the secretaries had reduced to writing the terms of the surrender, when the two commanders signed the instruments, after which there was a whispered conversation between Grant and Lee, which no one else but the two great chieftains heard. Then General Lee arose in that stately pride that seemed a part of the man, and bowed separately to each officer on the Federal side. Then, turning, he left the room, and striding down the garden in front of the house, bestrode the gray horse that had carried him through all the Virginia campaigns, and rode away.

When Lee had left the room, Grant called his officers about him, and then they learned the import of the whispered conversation, as the Federal chieftain said:

"General Lee's army is on the point of starvation, and we must assist them all we can. You," he said, naming an officer, "go to the Fifth Corps, and you to the Twenty-fourth," thus naming every corps, "and ask every man who has three rations to turn over two to the Confederates. Go to the commissaries and the quartermasters, and tell them to send all the food they can spare."

The orders were quickly obeyed, and before night 25,000 rations were carried to the Army of Northern Virginia.

As General Lee rode slowly back in silence, there gradually mingled with the deep sadness on his face a far-away expression, as if his thoughts were wandering to other scenes in that bloody drama, in which he had acted such a prominent part, and no words can express the humiliation that proud nature must have felt, as he met face to face the bitter end of all his hopes.

When early in the afternoon Lee had been seen riding toward the McLean house, the rumor of the surrender flew rapidly through the Confederate camp. And when, about 3 o'clock in the afternoon, he was seen slowly and thoughtfully riding back, it was known that the terms of surrender had been completed. Reaching his headquarters, he called his officers about him and explained to them the terms of the surrender. On hearing them they expressed their entire satisfaction at his course. The lines of battle, which had been drawn up awaiting a possible renewal of the conflict, were then broken, and eagerly the men crowded around their chief to clasp his hand. It was a touching scene, as they crowded around their old commander—under whom they had fought on many a bloody field for four long years—and expressed their love and confidence in him still. Many of their eyes were moist as they shook his hand and felt they were parting forever from their beloved chieftain. Sad indeed it was for those proud men, to hear that they could do no more, but furl their colors forever and go back to their shattered homes again; but in their simple words and actions there was something grand and noble, and their commander felt that there was no need of words of explanation, or vain regrets to such heroic men, as he said simply, while over his face came almost a womanly tenderness:

"Men, we have fought through the war together, and I have done the best I could for you."

* * * * *

On the 12th of April the Army of Northern Virginia had its last review, and as early as five o'clock on that morning a Federal division, under General Chamberlain, was formed in line of battle to receive the surrender of the arms and colors of the Confederates. The Federal line was nearly a mile in length, extending from the river bank along the streets of the village, almost to the court house. As they stood there they saw, through the morning mist, the Confederates breaking camp, and then slowly and reluctantly forming ranks for the last time. Then the Southern men wheeled into column of march and moved forward, with their battle flags, the stars and bars, flying. First came General Gordon, with Stonewall Jackson's corps, then Longstreet's corps, commanded by Heath. As the head of the Confederate column arrived opposite the Federal right, the bugle sounded, and the National troops presented arms, while their officers saluted. The Confederate commander, General Gordon, noticing this courteous recognition, also brought his men to a present and saluted with his sword. Then the Confederates wheeled into line of battle, and the two former contending armies *stood facing each other in peace for the first time and the last!*

Amid not the sound of a trumpet, nor the roll of a drum, but in a stillness as if the dead were passing there, the Southern soldiers stepped forward in squads and stacked their arms and took off their cartridge boxes and placed them in heaps. And last of all, they furled their battle flags, and as they laid them in the dust—the colors they had risked their lives so often to defend—they knelt down and kissed them, while their eyes filled with burning tears. It was a touching scene, and many a heart was full, even on the Federal side. Then only the stars and stripes waved over the field. Thus throughout the day the men of division after division marched forward and surrendered their arms, then after they had given their word of honor never to take up arms against their country again, they were set at liberty. Meanwhile, during that entire day not a cheer, not a taunt, not even a whispered boast of vain glory escaped from a single Federal soldier. For there came over the victors a tender feeling of almost brotherly friendship for their former foes, as they felt they were *fellow soldiers and fellow countrymen at last!*

In this last closing scene General Grant was not present, and with a tenderness that will ever be remembered by those vanquished men, he spared everything in his power that would wound their feelings, or that tended to imply the humiliation of a conquered foe. But, on the contrary, he received the surrender of the Southern men with a kind recognition that they were soon to be friends and countrymen again. Nor did General Grant's magnanimity end here, for he insisted that the private property of the Confederates should be respected, though the public property of the Southern army should be surrendered. And when asked if they should surrender their horses, he answered, "No, tell them to keep them; they will need them to plow their farms."

The Confederates, after having surrendered their arms and accoutrements, and taking the oath of allegiance, were allowed to roam at will. Then followed a remarkable scene, rarely if ever witnessed in the world's history before, victor and vanquished mingled in one great fraternal friendship, while the Federals divided with them their food, tobacco, etc. It was truly a wonderful scene of forgiving and forgetting.

There was one knot of soldiers collected near the right of the field, who would have especially attracted one's attention by their unusual jollity and good fellowship. And it needed but a single glance of the beholder to tell that they were former members of the Vandal Club. Some were in blue uniforms, others in gray, but national differences had no effect on their hilarity and friendship. In their midst stood Tom Gleaton, distributing the food in his knapsack, and at the same time discussing the edible qualities of sawdust pudding.

"Well," said a Vandal in gray, in answer to a question from Gleaton, "you know for the last two months we've been pretty hard up for food, in fact, we haven't had any at all. And the pangs of starvation have a very trying effect on a fellow's ingenuity, so when we came to an old saw mill, we resolved to make some sawdust pudding. We got some sawdust, stirred it up with water, put in some sugar, and baked it over a camp fire."

"Well, how did it eat?" asked Gleaton.

"It was a pretty tough dose. Little better than leather soup, but still it was better than nothing!"

At this moment the little group was joined by General Landon, who, after he had shaken hands with the Vandals in gray, distributed the food in his small bag among them, which was eagerly devoured.

"But," said Landon, in answer to their complaints, "didn't you have any meat?"

"Oh, once in a while we killed a mule, and I tell you it is wonderful how such small bits of meat stood so much chewing!"

At this juncture the men in gray were joined by a terrible hungry looking African, who, attracted by General Landon's bright shoulder straps, poked a Vandal in the back and whispered in his ear:

"Ax de General if he has food of any description 'bout his pusson."

"Hush up, Sambo," replied the Vandal, "do you think the General's a traveling cook-shop?"

"But he mought have a little extra bacon?" suggested the darkey.

"Hush up," said another Vandal, "you're always hungry."

The negro's pantomimic motions had not escaped Gleaton's observation, who said to Landon, "he's a terrible hungry looking African. The personification of starvation. I can tell by the drop of his under jaw."

"How about the size of his mouth?" suggested Landon.

"A fine opening for provisions."

General Landon had sent for a quantity of food, which now arrived, and the negro eagerly stepped forward to participate in the feast.

"Hold on," said Landon, with a merry twinkle in his eye, "you're an enemy, and it's against the laws of war to feed an enemy."

"I wuz, Massa General, but golly, I'ze loyal 'nough now."

"Well then, we'll have to feed you."

And soon the negro was devouring the food with great gusto, as he rolled the whites of his eyes about.

A Vandal in gray was cutting the rind off some bacon, when a pompous officer of the commissary general's staff passing exclaimed: "Young man, it has been customary heretofore to eat bacon rind and all."

"All right, old man," replied the Vandal, amid a roar of laughter, "*I'm cutting it off for you!*"

After the Vandals in blue and gray had shaken hands all around, they parted with the best of feelings toward each other, as Gleaton said, "Now we'll forgive past animosities, and sheath the sword, bury the hatchet, close the temple of Janus, furl the battle flag, smooth grim visaged war's wrinkled front, extend the olive branch, ——"

"And," added Landon, "smoke the calumet of peace."

"Thank you for the suggestion," replied Gleaton, "and if any of you don't happen to have a calumet about your person, a clay pipe will answer all practical purposes just as well."

"Here she is," said a Vandal, pulling out a short, black pipe.

Leaving the St. Arlyle group, General Landon walked down the Confederate line, eagerly scanning every knot of men in gray. At last his face lighted up with an unusual interest, as he caught sight of Ned Wilberton, the object of his search, and hurried toward him. As the two friends met, for the first time since the commencement of the war, they clasped hands in silence, with hearts too full for words. Landon was the first to break the silence, as he said, sympathetically:

"This is a sad ending for you, my dear fellow! And I am sincerely sorry for you, but perhaps it is for the best."

"I hope so," said Wilberton, sadly. "But I can't say so yet. But I hope some time, with God's help, to be able to do so. But my heart is too full of sorrow, and, I'm afraid, of bitterness also, to say so now. Yet I know it is the duty of a soldier and of a true man to bear no enmity against his former foe. Yet you know all it has cost me; more than my country, the life of her I held dearer than my heart's blood. But I know it would be her wish, if she were living, to speed the day of peace and friendship between the North and South, and so, with God's help, I shall try and fulfill her wish, on my humble part."

"Heaven bless you," said Landon, "and help you to bear your trials and afflictions. I know her death was a terrible blow to you, for she was as noble a girl as ever lived!"

After a short conversation the two friends parted, with hearts too full to longer trust themselves in each other's presence.

As General Landon walked onward he came to a clump of bushes in which a number of soldiers were collected. And there he saw one of the most touching sights—in its very pathetic sweetness—of all the sad scenes of war —the dead form of a little drummer boy of wondrous beauty. He was dressed in a full blue uniform, and as he lay he appeared like a dethroned statue of an Apollo. His face was as beautiful as a god's and as fair and delicate as that of a girl; his right arm grasped his drum and his left rested gently across his breast. He seemed rather as if sleeping, than dead. Kneeling beside him was another little drummer boy in gray—no larger than the other—endeavoring to pour water from a canteen between the white, cold lips, but his efforts were vain, for the little fellow had been dead for an hour or more.

It was a wonderfully affecting scene in its pure, tender pathos, and grim old warriors' eyes were wet, that had not been moist before for years.

After gazing in silence for several moments at the touching scene, General Landon said, as his voice grew husky with emotion:

"It is a sad sight, yet a beautiful omen of the lasting peace of the Republic, for it portends that the rising generation are forgiving and forgetting, ere the sounds of the conflict have died away."

Then, as Landon stepped forward and gently raised the little Confederate in his arms, he said, tenderly:

"My little fellow, you can do no more for him. He is dead!"

"Dead!" said the little drummer, as tears rolled down his cheeks. "*Dead!!* Will he never wake again?"

"No, my child," replied Landon, almost brokenly. Then the little fellow released himself from the young officer's grasp, and kneeling down by the dead boy, kissed him, as he said in his childish simplicity and faith: "Goodbye! God will take care of you now!" Then General Landon bore him away from the sorrowful scene.

The next day they rolled the little form in a blanket and buried it beneath a willow, with a cross above the grave, on which was carved the single word: "Harry."

On the morrow came the parting between the men of the former contending armies, and it was almost with a fraternal friendship that they bade each other farewell, for whoever began the war, and whatever their past differences might have been, they had fought the great battles together, and now they were *fellow soldiers together at last!*

Singly, in groups, on horseback and on foot, the Confederates left for their far-away homes, and the great Federal army was left supreme and alone. Then the Army of the Potomac faces northward, and receives its last orders before it begins its homeward march. As one of the adjutant-generals' assistants reads them he finishes with the following words:

"You will no longer be required to use the small tents, commonly called dog-tents (tents used in rapid marching) but you will be furnished with larger and better tents."

"Ah! that means," said Colonel Gleaton, pointing to the dog-tents with his sword, "that we're through with them to all *intents* and *purp-houses!*"

There was a burst of laughter from the men, while the officers shouted, "Silence in the ranks," though their own faces were wreathed in smiles.

Then the Federal army commenced its long march homeward. And it was dull and spiritless to those old soldiers to plod wearily along, without skirmishes ahead, and when they entered a valley to find no battery firing upon them from the heights beyond, but to feel they were a great army fully equipped for war, but without a foe.

Thus separated the two armies after four years of strife, and the men who met as foes parted at last as friends! They had learned to know each other better, and to love each other more, though the acquaintance had begun and ended on the blood-stained field of strife!

And now at last, through the dark, storm-lit clouds of war, were bursting the sweet beams of peace, like an angel of mercy heralding the happy sunshine of future years; while from the homes in every part of the broad Republic were going up prayers of thanks that the scenes of blood and death were nearly over!

CHAPTER XV.

THE LAST REVIEW OF THE ARMY OF THE POTOMAC.

"BRING out the flags before us,
  Unfurl them one by one;
Ere laid in solemn silence,
  Away from sight and sun,
With name and date of service,
  So men to come may read
How sped the loyal forces,
  When brave hearts took the lead."

THE clear, silvery sunshine of the 23d of May, 1865, was sweeping over Washington City, bathing the huge capitol with a crowning splendor, from its massive columns of dazzling whiteness to the very summit of the immense dome, that rested majestically on its massive stone base, like some giant monarch on his throne.

It was a day memorable for one of the great events in the closing scenes of the war—the last review and march of the Army of the Potomac.

Upon the broad expanse of Pennsylvania Avenue was drawn up in line the immense Army of the Potomac, numbering over 85,000 soldiers. It was the greatest display of martial strength the capital of the nation had ever yet witnessed, but as the morning sunbeams flashed on the gleaming arms of the long lines of men in blue, they fell for the last time on that proud army, for now its work was through.

Early in the day there was a slight commotion among those veteran soldiers, then the bugle sounded and the Army of the Potomac wheeled into column of march, and with General Mead riding proudly at its head, filed in long and stately array through the streets of Washington City, from the capitol past the presidential mansion. Upon a platform erected in front of the White House stood President Andrew Johnson, and by his side stood General Grant, the commander of the armies of the United States. Around these two central figures were grouped the judges of the Supreme Court, and the various officers of state.

Along the line of march immense crowds gazed upon the war-worn soldiers from every sidewalk, window, door-way and available house-top. Besides the thousands who had congregated through curiosity, were hundreds of men, women and children who had flocked to Washington City with beating hearts, to welcome back from the army brothers, husbands, sons and fathers they had not seen for years. And as they caught sight—from the windows or sidewalks—of the loved ones, the wild cries of delight and fluttering of handkerchiefs announced the fact, while the answering cheers from the ranks told that the joy was mutual.

No wonder those brave men's steps were light and their hearts were gay as they realized it was their *last march!* What words they were to them. They meant no more terrible marches under a hot southern sun, carrying heavy knapsacks. They meant farewell to tent and field and weary nights of picket duty. They meant an end to fields of blood and death, with the dangers of war leaving them crippled or dead. But, best of all, they meant a speedy reunion around the old hearthstones of home, amongst those they loved so dearly and tenderly.

Near the middle of the long column rode General Charlie Landon, at the head of his division, and at the rear of it came the St. Arlyle regiment, with Colonel Gleaton riding proudly at its head. Gleaton's explanation of the regiment being in the extreme rear was that it was not because the regiment was of the least importance, but, like the good things at a banquet, the best always came last.

As the regiment was passing a street corner, a delegation from St. Arlyle, who had come to welcome back their soldier-boys, caught sight of them and instantly broke into cheer after cheer. So wild was their enthusiasm that even Gleaton for several moments was so overcome by the sight of their joyous faces and their wild huzzas that he could only wave his hat. The situation had become trying, when a soldier and whilom member of the Vandal Club came to the rescue by slightly changing the old rallying cry on the battle field of Gettysburg: "We've come here to stay," to the words: "We're going home to stay!" Instantly the cry rang along the ranks: "We're going home to stay! We're going home to stay!"

By this time Gleaton had regained his composure, as he remarked:

"Yes, Othello's occupation's gone. So we'll beat our swords into plowshares, and our spears into pruning hooks, and go home to stay!"

At this juncture the regimental band struck up the strains of "Pat Malloy," and immediately the whilom Vandals in the ranks began singing over and over again the familiar lines:

"But now I'm going home again, as poor as I began,
To make a happy girl of Moll, and sure I think I can."

But instead of "Moll" they substituted various other girls' names, such as Belle, Nell, Em, etc. Perhaps these were the names of the sweethearts they had left behind them, but we will not try to pry into their private affairs.

At the end of the march the Army of the Potomac was drawn up in line once more, and the bands struck up their farewell strains, one near the center of the line playing the tune of "Roslyn Castle," the old air that had disbanded the Continental army at Newburgh, more than eighty years before. And as the final strains floated on the air the men broke ranks for the last time, and the great Army of the Potomac disappeared from view forever; though its memory will ever live in the hearts and affections of the country its soldiers fought so bravely to preserve.

As they heard the order to break ranks for the last time, and knew their toils and dangers were through, and felt that home and friends were near, it was a wonderful sight to see how differently these strong men expressed their delight. Thousands broke into wild cheers, while some were too overcome with happiness to speak, and stood like statues, as their eyes filled with joyous tears, as they felt they were near the realization of their greatest hopes and dreams!

A colonel, when he heard the order, sprang into the air, struck his heels together, and turned a complete somersault. And as he regained his feet he shouted: "Hurrah for Peace! I never loved you half as well as now!"

A large captain sprang forward, clasped his wife—who had come to meet him—in his arms, and as he lifted her off her feet and kissed her a dozen times or more, cried: "Emily, you've either grown smaller, or else my heart has grown bigger. I feel it's big enough to envelop a Colossus of Rhodes!"

"But," said Gleaton, who was standing behind him, "a pyramid, or perhaps old snowy-peaked Mount Blanc, might cool his ardor!"

A soldier had been standing calmly in the ranks, but when he heard the order to break ranks, his face lit up with an unusual brightness as he exclaimed, aptly and tersely, even above the tumult:

"Great Heavens! Those are the words I've been listening for, for the last four years. They mean wife, home and children!"

What a world of meaning there was in that soldier's simple words. It was the order the whole army had been hoping for after many a long campaign, and after many a desperate battle. In fact, it was the order for which the entire nation of heartsickened people was praying and longing.

But with the joys of Peace came the sad farewells between comrades forever. Comrades who for weary years had shared their common meals and tents together, or marched side by side through many a long campaign, or stood shoulder to shoulder on many a bloody field, or nursed and encouraged each other through sickness and wounds, till they were endeared to each other by almost family ties!

Then also came the soldiers' last tender parting from their commanders, the officers who had led them with noble example and encouragement while sharing their common dangers and sufferings too. Between none of the officers and the men was the parting more tender and sincere than between Charlie and the soldiers of his division. For there was a boyish frankness and generous good-heartedness about him that held a peculiar magnetism that very rarely failed to win its way to others' hearts. This, added to his dashing gallantry, his handsome face and fine commanding figure, and his brilliant flashes of conversation, showing his great depth of learning, and the easy, light and ingenuous way he had of imparting it, that won the attention and confidence of those about him, and above all, the sweet, tender expression that filled his eyes when his sympathies were aroused for a wounded soldier, or their daring glitter when facing a foe, that threw a charm about him few could resist.

At last the parting words were said, and the men scattered over the country to find rest in happy homes, surrounded by wife and children, or those they loved the best. And in the joys of peace and home old comrades were forgotten and forever separated, except to meet by chance, now and then, as they talked over the thrilling scenes they had passed through together. What a world of meaning there is in the word home! It means more than the house we inhabit; it means those we love the dearest and the best! And over Charlie Landon there came a feeling of sadness, as he felt he had no home in the truest sense of the word; for she he loved dearer than life was separated from him, perhaps forever! So in his grim despair he took charge of a geological expedition, to explore for six months in South America, in hopes that amid the new life his heart would lose some of the weary pain that was ever gnawing at it, for he felt he never could forget or control his love for her.

The next day after the review of the Army of the Potomac, General Sherman rode proudly through Washington City at the head of 150,000 sunburned and toil-worn soldiers, who had just returned from that long, remarkable march from Atlanta to the sea. And that day they broke ranks forever, and ere sunset that mighty army was only a thing of the past. And now again the stars and stripes floated in peace over the Republic, from its northern boundary to its extreme southern line. And may Heaven speed the day when time has calmed the sorrows and benumed the bitterness and regrets, and the heart is touched and softened by that tranquil and beautiful feeling, the memory of the dead—those brave soldiers in blue and gray, who fought for what they deemed the right—that feeling that arouses the better thoughts of our nature by the winning charm of sweet, pure sympathy, linked by the silver chord of memory and the golden chain of love to the everlasting world of peace; as if our souls had joined in mystic intercourse with the spirits of those across the waves of time!

Thus when the years have fallen, silent, calm and still—like the sunlight floods the globe—with an impartial touch on all, then will the laurels of victory have intertwined with the bliss of peace and love!

CHAPTER XVI.

SAD AND SWEET MEMORIES.

FRIENDS my soul with joy remembers!
  How like quivering flames they start,
When I fan the living embers
On the hearthstone of my heart.
—*Longfellow.*

LOWLY the train was moving out of Rome, on a beautiful afternoon in early June, as Bertha sat at an open car window, on her way to her native land. The golden summer sunlight was floating over the Eternal City in all its splendor, mingling with the clear, balmy Italian air, and as the train wound through the city, she caught last views of the rare old ruins and structures of ancient Rome, as they lay slumbering in the clear, warm air, while there thronged before her mental vision, scenes from their wondrous history, when Rome was the capital of the world. There before her view stood the gigantic Colosseum, within whose walls for ages were enacted brutal sports for the amusement of the Roman populace. Its huge interior, once capable of holding 80,000 people, and its massive walls, once towering high into the air, but now nearly half in ruins, yet amid the debris on the floor can still be found the bronze ring to which Christian martyrs and other cap-

lives were chained, while beneath the partly ruined spectators' galleries are still to be seen the vast ranges of cells where the wild beasts—panthers, tigers, leopards and lions—were kept that tore and mangled the human captives in mortal combat, while the multitude looked on and applauded.

"But," she thought, "what a change Christianity has produced! For there, where the dome of St. Peter's Cathedral looms high in the sky, were the gardens of Nero—the most cruel of all the Roman tyrants. It was there, during his reign, that the silent obelisks in the square before the cathedral witnessed the awful sights of human suffering. For it was there, on summer nights, that gay crowds—with the cruel Emperor among them—gathered to watch the ghastly human torches blacken the ground with pitch, while in each was a Christian martyr in his mantle of fire! And in the Colosseum near by, immense crowds were watching the purest of Christian men and women torn to pieces by wild beasts. No wonder, then, this gay capital—bathed as it was in human blood—met at last a terrible fate at the hand of the barbarian!"

Out of Rome the train wound slowly northward, through the Campagna, brilliant with the array of scarlet and yellow flowers, toward Florence, a hundred and fifty miles distant. And as she gazed from the car windows, it was a beautiful and entrancing sight that unfolded before her view, for this was Tuscany, the ancient Etruria of wondrous history. She catches glimpses of mountain heights, of cool, shady ravines, then of quaint old walled towns, slumbering in the dreamy, balmy Italian air. And there arises before her mind, as if by magic, visions of that glorious past recorded on the glowing pages of Arnold, Gibbon and Sesmondi. And farther back yet, her imagination wanders, ere Rome's regal and imperial glory was born, and while yet the lance and shield of the Middle Ages had more than two thousand years to wait, when the Etruscan commonwealth of twelve fair cities formed a confederacy that required all the early strength of Rome to subdue. And as the train whirls along, there passes like a panorama the ruins of these cities of bygone glories and the tombs of Porsena and Lucomo and the other heroes of that departed age, sleeping unconscious of the two thousand years and more of history that has since elapsed.

And again her thoughts sweep over those later years, when Tuscany was bathed in blood, successively by the Roman rulers, the Gothic conquerors, and the Frankish and the German warriors, but on whose gallant deeds the curtain of the past has fallen forever. Thus under the effects of the warm, balmy air, a dreamy languor had stolen over her, when suddenly she was aroused from her reverie, just as the train was leaving a little sleepy Italian station, by a gentle tap on the shoulder. Instantly her thoughts, which had floated far away into time and space, were brought back to the consciousness of the present.

Bertha looked up, and with a start of surprise she saw Colonel Edward Wilberton standing by her side. Over her lovely face there came an expression of pleasure, mingled with sadness, as she thought, "now I shall hear of poor, dear May's death, and"—with a slight blush—"of Charlie Landon too."

After they had exchanged a few words of greeting, he seated himself by her side in silence. For over the minds of each, rolled a flood of memories of those stirring bygone years—sad and tender thoughts, that seemed almost too deep for words.

At last, Bertha, with a woman's gentleness and tact, broke the silence with a commonplace question and quickly and skillfully led to the subjects nearest her heart.

"How long have you been in Italy?" she asked.

"About two months," he replied. "Are you going to Florence?"

"Yes," she answered, "on my way home to America. For I shall ever consider it home, for around it cling the dearest and sweetest memories of all!"

"It will also," he said, "be home to me, though I fought against its flag. But it cost me dearly; all that I loved tenderest in this world. And my severe chastening, I think, has gone far toward atoning for my willfulness. And though my heart at first was filled with a bitter desire for revenge, time has calmed and mollified it, and my wishes now are for the welfare of the whole country. For I feel it holds the grave of her I loved better than all the world beside. My noble, true-hearted May."

"Sweet, gentle May!" exclaimed Bertha, as her dark eyes grew moist. It seems so cruel that war's rude hand should have claimed her as one of its victims. She, whose every thought was one of love for others, and whose every deed seemed an act of kindness for those around her. But I'm sure her faith, like her life, was perfect to the last!"

"Indeed it was. And her last wishes, like the acts and thoughts of her life, were for the welfare of those she loved. For even the approach of Death's cold, icy hand could not still her loving heart, till it had ceased to beat!"

"She was mortally wounded at Gettysburg?" said Bertha, as her beautiful dark eyes grew wet with tears.

"Yes," he replied, as over his face came an almost womanly tenderness, mingled with sadness. He then gave a graphic description of May's tragic death.

"But," he continued, "before her noble, loving heart was stilled forever she said:

"'Tell Bertha, when you see her, that my last moments were calm and happy. And tell her to crush her pride, and be true to her own heart and Heaven will bless her.'"

"God bless her," said Bertha, "if He can, more than He already does in her happy home in Heaven," she continued, as the tears filled her dark eyes and fell upon the fragrant blossoms on her bosom, while there came a wonderful tenderness over her lovely face.

"May grew rapidly weaker," Wilberton continued, "as she said with a strong effort: 'Good-bye, Ned! Don't cry! We've had a happy life together. It seems hard to go, yet God's will be done. But I shall meet you on the shining shore of Peace!'

"Then her arm tightened convulsively and passionately around my neck, and her sweet blue eyes sought mine with a last, wild, loving glance! Then the little hand relaxed its hold on my neck, and the eyelids drooped heavily forever over the sweet blue eyes! I bent my head quickly and kissed her lips, as with her parting breath 'the light of immortal beauty silently covered her face.' Then as my head sank upon her breast, I heard the last beat of her heart, and I knew the rosy lips would never smile upon me again, and that the sweet blue eyes would *never greet me more!*

"Like one in some horrible dream, I saw the last rays of twilight solemnly fade, and darkness shroud the Pennsylvania hills; and sad and gloomy it fell upon me! In that long, sorrowful night that closed around me, there sprang forth grim spectres of sweet memories, hopes and loves, that haunted me but to remind me that they were dead, till there came upon me a feeling of desolation, like one lost forever in a dark wilderness; as I realized that my brightest hopes, dreams and wishes were shattered forever! And in that awful night there sprang out of the darkness many vivid scenes of suffering and agony, till I felt like the lost soul in the old Greek mythology, as it is borne by the ghastly ferryman, Charon, across the Stygian River!

"There, long after midnight, they found me, still clasping her inanimate form! They bore her form into camp, and I followed, like one in some horrible dream. I had all that was mortal of her buried in St. Arlyle. Then I joined my regiment again, with a heart maddened with anger, and with a thirst for revenge *no words can express!* And I resolved to fight the war out to the *bitter end!* Though I scarcely cared to know—so deep was my desire for vengeance—what that end would be!"

"The battle of Gettysburg," continued Wilberton, "was the turning point of the war, but we fought on as desperately as ever. After that battle, we had one more chance for victory, on the terrible battle field of the Wilderness. But we failed, and after that we saw the star of Confederacy gradually but surely sinking, until it disappeared forever on an April day, on the field at Appomattox, nearly a year later!

"During the last battles around Richmond we were reduced to but eight thousand men, while the great Federal army numbered nearly two hundred thousand, but we struggled on with a bravery that surprised the enemy, and with a success at resistance that even astonished us. But what the result would be of that last protracted struggle, was as evident to the commonest soldier as it was to the commander himself—it meant *annihilation* or surrender! But those few men of that once great army of Northern Virginia were fighting with a desperation akin to death, for most of them had lost their all—and in the grimness of despair they little cared what the end would be! The end came on an April day, when we stacked our arms forever, and laid our colors in the dust! But the end was a surprise to us, for we found the Federal soldiers wonderfully kind and tender. They gave more than a generous half of their food to our starving men, and they endeavored in every way not to hurt our feelings, or to make us feel like a humiliated foe. For, said they, have we not fought the great battles together, and are we not *fellow soldiers at last?* And in those few days we learned to know and like them better than we ever had before!"

"I was standing," continued Wilberton, "on the field of surrender, when Charlie Landon came to me with his old winning, boyish frankness, and as he grasped my hand, he said with a kind expression on his handsome face and a tenderness in his voice that won my heart:

"'This is a sad ending, my dear fellow! And I am sincerely sorry for you, but it is perhaps for the best?'"

"He is," continued Wilberton, "a noble fellow; generous, true and kind; incapable of a mean action or word; for he has a heart as far above meanness and envy as the heavens are above the earth. He is the most brilliant scholar I ever knew, for so young a man. He is a noble, generous soldier, and as brave as a lion! In fact, he has just the qualities of a hero. For I have met him as a foe, and tried him as a friend, and he realizes in all its fullness the poet's line of 'Truest friend and noblest foe.'"

Bertha looked up, as a blush mantled her beautiful face, and the lovelight sparkled in her dark, velvety orbs, as she said:

"You are very generous in the praise of your friends."

"Not always," he said. "But in my admiration of Charlie Landon I am only just, for he deserves it all, and more."

After a moment's silence, Wilberton continued: "So Charlie Landon and I parted, but I hope ere long to meet him again, in a united country. For one of my greatest wishes now, is to see my country united in hearts as well as bonds. One of the great philosophers, and wise men of Greece was once asked: 'What is the most grateful of all things?' and he answered, '*Time*.' His answer was a very true one; for time is a great softener of asperities, as well as a corrector of judgments. For though, even now, when I catch sight of the stars and bars, there arises a tender, true memory of the stormy days when I rallied under its folds, still when I see the stars and stripes, there arises the love of my boyhood and early manhood, and older and dearer love even still!"

"And," said Bertha, archly, "old loves are always the strongest and the best!"

"True," he replied, smiling. "I have found it so, for there were moments in the early days of the Civil War when, as I looked across the battle line and saw the old flag floating there, I almost felt as Homer depicts the feelings of Helen, while she gazed from the ramparts of Troy, as with 'former fires'

"'Her country, parents, all that once were dear,
Rush to her thoughts, and force a tender tear.'

"For it was the flag of my boyhood, of my early manhood, too, and the tenderest impulses of my heart still clung to the dear old flag, *for under its folds the sweetest years of my life had been passed*, when 'Hope was life's sweet sovereign, and the heart and step were light.'"

At last the fair city of Florence dawns in view, that Tuscan lily, which Italy wears like a blossom upon her breast. And in that lovely June afternoon, the beautiful city lay shining in the sunlight like a gem in a beautiful setting of green. They catch sight of the many gilded palaces, and watch the sunlight glitter on the immense dome of the Duomo, and flash in fiery corruscations from the hundreds of spires of that wonderful city. And while they yet gaze in admiration, the Angelus bells, of the world-famed Cathedral of Campanile, peal forth their sweet melody on the perfumed air

—arising from the array of flowers of every hue—sending forth, as it were, a double welcome to the fair, ancient city.

"This is my station," said Colonel Wilberton, arising as the train approached a small station. "Do you intend to tarry in Florence?"

"No, I am going home to the United States," she replied, smiling, *"for despite the sunny skies of Italy, my heart is roving there!* For I never loved my country better than I do now. And," she added, as a warm tint mantled her lovely face, and a beautiful light filled her dark, lustrous eyes, "one of the greatest wishes of my heart is to see the men who wore the blue and gray, mingled in as perfect fellowship as the gray dawn of a summer morning is mingled with the perfect blue of a summer day."

"And I think the omens are propitious toward realizing your wish," he replied, with a smile. "For a short time before I left America, I went over the old battle fields, and I found, just as the North and South were forgiving and forgetting, so nature, too, was hiding the old scars of enmity, and the lilies of love and peace were springing *where the laurels used to grow!* For on the field of Gettysburg, the Federal and Confederate monuments of valor are standing *almost side by side!"*

CHAPTER XVII.

THE VANDAL CONGRESS ONCE AGAIN.

SEE a chief who leads my chosen sons,
All armed with points, antitheses and puns.
—*Pope.*

AFTER the close of the Civil War, and the return of the absent Vandals to St. Arlyle, the Vandal Club, or Congress, (as they themselves called it) was reorganized and placed in a more flourishing condition. Although during the War its organization had been continued, the Club had gradually lost one member after another, until the interest in it had sunk to a very low ebb. But with the return of the old members and the addition of new ones, there came a new era in its prosperity, until, to use the words of Gleaton, "it transcended its pristine glory."

An adjunct that had materially assisted in increasing its membership was the rapid growth of the village, since it had become a popular bathing resort. The Club had so far progressed toward placing its organization on a permanent basis as to be able to build a club house on the lot which they had purchased. The source from which the Vandals had obtained their funds was at first somewhat enveloped in mystery, but it gradually became known that several prominent persons had assisted them. Among the number was Richard Lex, who had been elected a county judge, for he had become a sober and useful citizen. Colonel Tom Gleaton had also sent them a present of fifty dollars. Charles Landon had, to use their own words, "kindly interested himself in their affairs, and materially assisted them with pecuniary emoluments." And last to be mentioned, but not least in giving, was Miss Bertha Merton, who had not forgotten how intimately they were intertwined with those troublous days of the past, and how nobly and manfully they had come to her assistance. Her gifts consisted of money and books, both of which they received with many thanks, expressed by means of the most grandiloquent letters the Club could compose, which when she read she would remark with a smile that "they are good fellows and deserving of encouragement, though somewhat addicted to compliments and high flown language."

As we have remarked, one of Miss Merton's gifts consisted of books, and this formed the nucleus of their constantly increasing library. Their library was a heterogeneous collection of works on law, science, literature and philosophy. Pre-eminent among their books were several full sets of encyclopedias and three large dictionaries. These latter volumes, they claimed, were very essential to the Congress' progress, as we shall also see if we attend a session of the Club.

It was Saturday night, and the Vandal Congress was in full session. There are many changes in their ranks since last we chronicled their proceedings, but still we recognize many familiar faces—grown older, it is true—but still with the same felicitous, jolly expression on them as of yore.

It was a large room, and extending entirely across the floor, were rows of chairs, in which the members ensconced themselves during a session. Facing the chair, and against the wall, was a raised platform, covered by a crimson plush canopy, and on this dais was a large arm chair, which was occupied by the President during their deliberations. Directly in front of this platform were two desks, where the two secretaries sat who recorded the proceedings of the Congress. On one side of the room was a huge desk, piled with books and papers, at which the reference clerk sat, whose duties we shall learn of by and by. The walls, where not occupied by book cases, were covered with pictures, maps and charts. In one corner of the room stood a glass case, filled with minerals, swords, belts, guns, balls, and various other souvenirs of the War. In another corner stood a large brass-knobbed wooden safe, painted green, on which was delineated in vivid colors, a huge bull dog—evidently the Cerberus of the treasury. What the safe contained was a mystery—for it was very heavy and was never opened—but the tradition ran that it was filled with bricks.

The Club had elected a new President, named Samuel Verbum, who was remarkable for two characteristics, his great and grandiloquent command of language and his sempiternal ability to smoke an immense pipe. He seemed to be acquainted with all the words in the dictionary, and to be able to use them on any occasion with a volubility that was wonderful. But a new or rare word was his delight, and he caught it in a moment and enfolded in his tenacious memory with a grip like Nessus's shirt on the body of Hercules.

During the session of the Club Verbum smoked the huge pipe, with a bowl the size of a teacup, into which he would pour a quarter of a pound of tobacco, and then, seating himself in the President's chair, would puff forth immense volumes of smoke, like a human steam engine. It was said that he only smoked during a meeting of the Club, but anyhow it was on these occasions alone he smoked the immense pipe. Several Vandals, in Sam's absence, had surreptitiously obtained the meerschaum, and after filling it with tobacco, had endeavored to smoke it, but after nearly killing themselves, had yielded to him the palm as a smoker, just as they had long since admitted him to be the chief in the use of rare words and grandiloquent language.

Samuel Verbum was reporter on the village paper. He was of medium height, about twenty-two or three years of age, with a full, good-natured face, brown eyes, dark, wavy hair, a black, curling moustache, and—in opposition to the prevalent idea of a hard student—a full, rounded figure, for, notwithstanding Sam's hard study in devouring an English unabridged dictionary and most of a standard encyclopedia, he had literally grown fleshy during his great feast of words. Those members of the Vandal Club who had entered the army, had found Sam in another regiment in their brigade, or perhaps he had discovered them, or, rather, the discovery was mutual, for he had affiliated with them as instinctively as a duck takes to water. He had obtained his transfer from his regiment to their company, and at the close of the war he had drifted back with them to St. Arlyle.

As we have remarked, it was Saturday night, and the Congress was in full session. It was a grand occasion, being their first gala meeting since the War, and there were present by invitation a number of ex-Vandals, among others Colonel Tom Gleaton. These invited guests were to make a few remarks, to give *"eclat,"* as the Vandals expressed it, to the occasion. After Samuel Verbum had taken the chair and sent forth a few huge puffs of smoke from his immense meerschaum, he called the meeting to order and requested the clerk to call the roll and read the minutes of the last session, after which he announced:

"We will now proceed to the profluent order of business, and the secretary will peruse the communication addressed to the Vandal Congress."

The secretary then read a brief communication from Miss Merton, tendering a gift of a hundred dollars to the Vandal *Club*.

"It should be addressed to the Vandal *Congress*," said Verbum. "What is the sense of the assembly?"

"Suspend the rules and accept the donation," moved a member.

"But that will not assist us," said Verbum. "It is not according to parliamentary usages."

"Suspend the name, and take in the appropriation," shouted a Vandal.

And the name was according suspended, and the appropriation taken in. A resolution of thanks to Miss Merton was then offered and unanimously adopted, after it had undergone numerous emendations and additions, until it was invested with the most grandiloquent language possible.

"She is," said Verbum, referring to Miss Merton, "a noble little lady, and in the words of the Roman proverb, *Autor pretiosa facit*—the giver makes the gift more precious."

"Yes," said Ed Thorne, the reference clerk, "she is an example of the Latin apothegm, *Gratior ac pulchro veniens in corpore virtus*, which we may freely translate: Beauty lends grace even to intrinsic worth."

"She fulfills," said Joe Percival, the philosopher of the Club, "the ancient sage's definition that 'Beauty is a sovereignty that stands in need of no guards.'"

"And also," said Will Anderson, "Aristotle's definition of beauty: 'The gift of a fair appearance.'"

"To see her," said Joe Percival, "and to wonder why all praise her, is to exclaim with Aristotle, when some one asked him 'why all people admire beauty.' 'Why,' he exclaimed, 'it is the question of a blind man!'"

"Or," said a member near the door, "to use the words of Plato, 'Beauty is the privilege of nature,' and in the words of Theocritus, 'An ivory mischief,' and in those of Socrates, 'A short lived tyranny.'"

There was instantly cries of dissension and hisses, while over Verbum's face came an expression of surprise and anger, as he exclaimed: "Sergeant-at-arms, carefully eliminate that member from the assembly!"

The sergeant-at-arms seized his huge stuffed club, nearly as large as himself, and instantly made a charge on the obnoxious member, who was endeavoring to escape, but the club came in contact with his posterior and elevated him about ten feet into the street. As the officer of order closed the door he exclaimed:

"In the words of the Bard of Avon, 'How are we tossed on Fortune's fickle flood!'"

"Nothing in this world," said President Verbum, as he rapped for order, "excels a fool with too long a tongue!

"'Nothing exceeds in ridicule no doubt,
A fool in fashion, but a fool that's *out*.'"

"No one," said Will Johnson, "but an idiot would make such frivolous remarks about a young lady who has been such a true friend to the members of this body. She is a noble little lady. I saw her the other day, and she looked irresistibly and bewitchingly beautiful, without a thought of the entrancing thrill she sent darting through many a fellow's heart!"

As the last speaker finished, Verbum gave a long puff on his large pipe, then laid it aside for a crowning effort, as he began:

"She's a dainty, bewitching little lady; she's a charming, bonny girl; she's a sweet, darling little maid; she's as beautiful as a Hebe, as lovely as a Venus, as graceful as a Peri, as fair as a lily, and as dazzling as a goddess! She's truly gorgeous, superb, magnificent, sublime, grand! In a sentence, she realizes the artist's fancy, and the poet's dream, when he wrote:

"'When life looks lone and dreary,
What light can expel the gloom?
When Time's swift wing grows weary,
What charm can refresh his plume?
'Tis woman, whose sweetness beameth
O'er all that we feel and see,
And if man of heaven e'er dreameth,
'Tis when he thinks purely of thee.'"

When Verbum ceased speaking there was a silence for several moments, broken at last by the President asking: "Has anyone anything more to add?"

"I think not," said Thorne, as he gazed in despair at the ponderous volumes before him. "I guess you've nearly tested the power of the English language."

"Are there any other communications?" asked Verbum.

"Yes," replied the clerk, reading one from the trustees of the town library, asking for a donation of books.

"It seems to me," said Verbum, "that charity should inaugurate proceedings on its own native heath. But I merely throw this out as a supererogatory, metaphysical suggestion. What are the wishes of the assembly?"

"I move," said a member, "that the communication lie on the table." And it was accordingly tabled.

"There being no other messages before the house," said the President, "we will now take cognizance of the protocol of the chairman of the committee on 'News About Town.'"

"In our last report," began Will Stoakes, "we gave an account of an attempt by some of the musically inclined boys to whip the clergyman, and also the outcome. But we were unable at that time to state the cause of the belligerent attitude of the parties. It seems, a short time ago the St. Arlyle amateur brass band attended the funeral of one of the firemen, and when they had squelched out, at the side of the grave, what they called 'The Sweet By and By' in a tune that resembled a cross between the howl of a hyena and the whine of a dying pup (in fact it was such a dismal discord that several persons in the rear looked over the others' shoulders to see what kind of an animal they were torturing) the minister in his address said that 'the deceased was, in one respect, fortunate in being thus called early.' That was all he remarked, but a great many people grinned, and the amateur 'wind-jammers' said that his infernal sarcasm was entirely out of place at a funeral."

"Perhaps," said Ed Thorne, "the minister merely threw it out as a supererogatory, metaphysical suggestion."

"Maybe he did," replied Stoakes, "but the 'wind-jammers' felt exceedingly warlike about it, and called upon the minister, with the results we have already related."

"There arrived in town, about three months ago," continued Stoakes, "a verdant appearing fellow, who looked as if he had been browsing among the chaparral on some mountain side. A few days since, he requested to be admitted into the Vandal Congress. So we told him that we would initiate him, and accordingly we took him up into Kirkman's warehouse. We told him there were four degrees, the highest of which was the Royal Skyfogle degree, which was very difficult to take, and that few people were able to take it. His answer was: 'Bring along your degrees; I'll take 'em!' After we had read to him the printed ritual of the Free Masons, Odd Fellows, and other secret societies, we blind-folded him, and leading him into a closet we let the old skeleton drop on him. He gave a howl like a scared wolf, and it was all we could do to hold him. Then we took him out of the closet and blind-folded him again, and from our past experience we thought it best to tie his hands behind his back. Then we drew him over a table, and while two of us held him by the ears the other one paddled him with a board. He laid it on well, and the victim howled to a lively tune. Then we let him wander around the warehouse, and fall over a dozen boxes and barrels, till he had skinned his shins and his nose. Then we caught him, and laying him on a table, held him by the ears while we gave him some more paddling, after which we dipped his head in a bucket of water, then in a box of flour, and finally in a box of powdered charcoal, when he looked like a cross between an African and an albino. Then we untied his hands and took the bandage from his eyes, and the first question he asked was:

"'Am I a Vandal now?' We told him 'yes.'

"'And have I taken the Royal Skyfogle degree?' We told him he had taken the Royal Skyfogle degree.

"'Then, boys," said he, 'I'll initiate you in the thunder and lightning degree, and make you eat humble pie!'

"And with that remark he knocked me down, he hit Dave Johnson in the eye and Ed Thorne in the jaw. When we all arose from the floor, we closed in with him. I seized him by one arm, Dave got him by the other, and Thorne seized him by the leg. The first thing he did, he kicked Dave in the stomach and doubled him up like a jack-knife, he threw me about ten feet, and pitched Ed head-first into the barrel of charcoal. Then he seemed satisfied, and we were very glad of it, for we like to see a man satisfied.

"He proved a great surprise to us. But, in the words of the old proverb: 'You can't always tell by the size of the toad how far he can jump!'"

"Yes," said Verbum, "there is a great deal of truth in the Roman proverb, *Fronti nulla fides*—there is no trusting to appearances."

At this juncture one of the Vandals, who was standing in the doorway holding a whispered conversation with some one outside, advanced to the middle of the room and raised his hand, to attract the President's attention.

"Mr. Brown has the floor," said Verbum.

"There's a nigger out there," said the member, with a jerk of his thumb over his shoulder, "who wishes to be admitted to the floor. He says he was in the war."

"That is not the way to speak, sir. You should say 'gentleman of color.'"

"Yes, he's got the color, for he's as black as the ace of spades!"

"What is the wish of the assembly?" asked Verbum.

"Admit him!" shouted the members, who had a penchant for anyone who had served in the war.

The negro entered, and as he took a seat and gazed at Verbum in wonder, he exclaimed: "Golly! don't he smoke a big pipe!"

Then President Verbum, without noticing his remark, began to interrogate him as follows:

"What is your name?"

"James Cæsar, sah."

"Where were you born?"

"In Norf Carolina, sah."

"How long were you in the war?"

"Nine months, sah."

"Where were you? In what army, I mean."

"I wuz five months in de hospital, sah."

"Where were you the other four months?"

"I wuz—I wuz looking for de hospital, sah."

"Sergeant-at-arms!" shouted Verbum, "carefully eliminate the gentleman of color from this assembly."

The sergeant-at-arms sat his huge stuffed club by the door, and then went for the darkey, and as he caught him by the ear, he said in a stage whisper: "Come Mr. Cæsar! Get! Skip! Shake a leg! Make your conge!" He led the blackamoor to the door, and seizing his club, he gave him a blow in the rear that hoisted him a dozen feet into the street.

As the colored gentleman gathered himself out of the dust, he exclaimed:

"Golly! Boss, dat wuz a terrible *hist!* But I'll clean out de whole institution!"

"In the words of Homer," said Verbum, "'Thy aid we need not, and thy threats defy.' And I hope your conge is a supererogatory, metaphysical suggestion that no imposters can foist themselves upon this body."

CHAPTER XVIII.

THE VANDAL CONGRESS, CONTINUED.

> YES, we're boys—always playing with tongue or with pen!
> And I sometimes have asked, Shall we ever be men?
> Shall we always be youthful, and laughing. and gay,
> Till the last dear companion drops smiling away?
> Then here's to our boyhood, its gold and its gray!
> The stars of its winter, the dews of its May!
>
> —*O. W. Holmes.*

"THE report of the Chairman of the Hymeneal Committee is now in order," said Verbum.

Pete Hale began : " Mr. President: During the past week there have been several marriages, or, to express it more poetically, several youths and maidens have caught the ethereal fragrance of love, or, to use the words of Homer, have themselves been caught by the 'The old, yet still successful cheat of love.'

"The first marriage of the week we have to chronicle is that of Sam Dawn to Mary Black. Sam Dawn first fell in love with Nellie Edwards, and they became engaged, but it was the old story, the course of true love didn't run smooth. At first the subtle aroma of romance clung around their betrothment, and in their blissful imaginations they seemed to live in a delightful dream. But alas! the awakening came. They began by a few lovers' quarrels, and ended by breaking the engagement. I am not philosopher enough to tell why, but it is a fact that love is nearly always associated with misery. Especially is this true of the younger loves—what are denominated first loves. The boy falls in love, and there is but one great object in the universe for him,—a girl's fair, sweet face—and it dazzles him with its luster, wherever he may roam. He feels that he has entered a new world, and the light of that face dazzles his eyes. Then he is absent a few weeks, and on his return he finds a change in his sweetheart, and they quarrel, and she tells him that she has found some one she loves better. And his idyllic dream, with its sweet, tender memories, is shattered forever! And he feels that ruin and chaos have closed around all things, and that the world is a deception. Though his friends may ridicule his pain, and he may reason with himself till he thinks he has completely conquered the old pain, yet the sight of her fair face, or the scent of the perfume that always seemed to cling about her may in a moment make his heart swell with all its old bitterness again. But after awhile he becomes disenamored, and then becomes a misogynist for awhile, but finally he recovers, and then he discovers that there are other fair faces in the world, for, as the poet says:

'Ay, such is man's philosophy when woman is untrue,
The loss of one but teaches him to make another do.

"And Sam Dawn met Mary Black, and she proved a balm for nearly all his woe, and so you see, to slightly change the old proverb, ''Tis always the Blackest just before the Dawn.'

"The next marriage we have to report is that of James King to Nelly Slave. They are of a nubile age and new people in the village, and we have not been able to learn much about them; but in the words of the poet:

'Love! thou art not a King alone;
Both *Slave* and *King* thou art.
Who seeks to sway, must stoop to own
The Kingdom of the heart.'

"It is with pleasure," continued Hale, "that we announce the marriage of Charles Havens to Emily Thorne, for it is the consummation of a lifelong love. He is generous, brave and handsome; a man and a scholar, with a noble, tender and true heart, that the girl who has won it must dearly prize. His genial manner, his goodheartedness, and his true friendship, while seemingly unconscious of it all, have won for him every true heart's admiration.

She is a charming, accomplished little brunette, with a sweet, winning way. She is a noble little lady, with a warm, pure heart, an originality about her that is ever fresh and pure, while her sunny smile and sympathy have won the love of young and old. And to him who has won her she is more than a golden prize, for she is a treasury of sympathy, courage and love!

"And undoubtedly they have both realized their ideals; he in the fair, sweet girl, with a noble heart; and she in the man who, despite the world's sordid touch, still possesses a bright record, without a blot! And may he long realize the sweetness of the lines:

'Oh, pleasant is the welcome kiss,
When the day's dull round is o'er,
And sweet the music of the step
That meets us at the door.'

"There is," continued Hale, "a prospective marriage on the tapis, that of our esthetic friend Fred Stone to a city girl. I saw him out buggy riding with his inamorata the other day, driving a piebald horse, and as the poet says:

'I saw the curl of his waving lash,
And the glance of his knowing eye,
And I knew he thought he was cutting a dash,
As his steed went thundering by.'"

As Pete Hale finished speaking, there came a series of loud raps at the door, and the sergeant-at-arms hastened to it. When he opened the door and gazed out, there came over his face a strong expression of surprise, which each moment increased, as he dropped his club and his eyes and his mouth opened in wonder to their full extent. Then, recovering his self-possession, he flung the door wide open, and in stepped Professor Phantom, tall, gaunt, grim, ghostly as ever! In an instant every member of the Club was on his feet in amazement, for it had been reported that Phantom had died, and had been buried nearly a year before; in fact, several persons in the village claimed that they had attended his funeral. When the Vandals recovered from their momentary surprise they eagerly crowded around Phantom, and as they shook hands with him they greeted him with such expressions as: "How are you, Ghost?" "Hello, Goblin! What's the news from Hades?" "How are you, Professor Spook? You're the same old rattlebones." "Why, you're as fat as a match!" and numerous similar expressions. But Phantom bore their railery and gibes good-naturedly, and even seemed pleased at their hearty welcome. When order had been restored, Phantom said:

"Mr. President and members of the Vandal Congress: It is with a world of pleasure that I receive your kindly greeting, and my heart tells me that I am again among friends. Life has many trials and vicissitudes, but I feel, to use a classical phrase, *Post tot naufragia portum* — after many shipwrecks, I have found a harbor. I am growing old, and cannot bear the fluctuating tide of fickle fortune, as in former years. And I am aware that the rejuvenescence of youth has departed, and I shall never begin in the incipiency of things again."

"No," said Verbum, "when nature makes a miscalculation, she never repeats the identical experiment, at least not with the same material."

"Exactly," said Phantom, "and I'm content to say, in the words of the poet:

'Fortune and Hope, farewell! I've gained the port;
You've fooled me long — make others now your sport.'"

"Or, in the words of Homer," replied Verbum:

'The field of combat fits the young and bold;
The solemn council best becomes the old.'"

"Very appropriate, Mr. President, very appropriate!"

"I merely threw it out as a supererogatory, metaphysical suggestion."

"I move," said a Vandal, "that Professor Phantom be elected a member of the Vandal Congress."

"He was a whilom member, was he not?" asked Verbum.

"Yes," replied the clerk, after he had examined the roll.

"Then he is already a Vandal. For, like the College of Cardinals, once a Cardinal, always a Cardinal, so it is with this body, once a Vandal, always a Vandal. Only the King of Terrors can remove a member."

At this moment a card was sent in from the door, bearing a request to see Verbum. He immediately called Will Stoakes to the chair and left the room.

As Verbum left the room Ed Thorne arose and said: "Mr. President: I was never so surprised in my life as when I saw our illustrious friend Professor Phantom enter the room, after so many of our citizens had attended his funeral, and it reminds me forcibly of a story, which runs as follows:

"Two sailors with a tame parrot one night went to a sleight of hand show, held in the upper part of a warehouse, in New Orleans. Although the three constituted the entire audience, the showman proceeded with the performance. He was very clever, and performed some very wonderful tricks, so that he greatly excited the amazement of one of the sailors, who after every feat of jugglery would exclaim:

"'That's pretty good! I wonder what he'll do next?'

"After awhile the silent sailor asked leave to smoke his pipe, which was granted, 'seeing,' as the magician remarked, 'there were no ladies present.' Thus the performance proceeded, one of the sailors smoking his pipe in silence, while the other would exclaim after every trick:

"'That's pretty good! I wonder what he'll do next?'

"At last the sailor of few words grew tired of smoking, and knocked the hot ashes from his pipe through a knot-hole in the floor, all unconscious that four hundred tons of gunpowder were stored below!

"In an instant they were all, with the exception of the parrot, blown to the kingdom to come. The parrot was blown about three miles into the air and across the Mississippi River, where it came down with the loss of its wings, one eye and a leg, while its tail feathers were burned off. As the bird flopped down on a post on its only remaining leg, it shrieked wildly:

"'That's pretty good!! I wonder what he'll do next?'"

Just as Thorne concluded his narrative Verbum entered, and in answer to Stoakes's offer to vacate the chair, he said: "No, retain the chair; I wish to make a few remarks. I was never so astonished in my life," he began, "as when our quondam and illustrious compatriot, Professor Phantom, appeared before us. That mortal man could appear again after so many of the denizens of our village had attended his obsequies, and after the Vandal Congress had given him such a brilliant obituary, is astounding to a marvelous degree! And I can only portray my wonderment by the ensuing apologue, which with the acquiescence of this august body, I will will proceed to annunciate:

"Two mariners, accompanied by a domesticated scansorial avis, on a nocturnal occasion, attended an exhibition of the Theurgic art in the metropolis of New Orleans. Although they constituted the entire audience, nevertheless the nomadic prestidigitator inaugurated proceedings in the esoteric science. The disciple of magic eventuated to very expert and dædalian, in performing remarkable mysticism, so that he engendered the prodigious amazement of one of the sons of Neptune, who, subsequent to every conguration, would vociferate:

"'Trismegistus! but that trenches on the admirable. My curiosity becomes procreated to become cognizant of what he will effectuate in the futurity?'

"Subsequently the taciturn mariner solicited permission to produce the ebolition of a jag of tobacco in his chiboque, as it was his assuetude to do, which, owing to the fair daughters of Eve being reduced to nihility, was accordingly conceded. Thus proceeded the concutenation of events in the accrescent mystical seance, one of the sons of Neptune performing an ebo..-

tion on his nargile, or dudeen, while the other vociferated in the sequel of each prestidigitation:

"'Trismegistus! but that trenches on the admirable. My curiosity becomes procreated to become cognizant of what he will effectuate in the futurity?'

"By way of a denouement, or finale, the pauciloquent sailor became surfeited with the ebolition of tobacco, and insidiously collided the glowing embers from his calumet, through an aperture in the floor, unaware of the existence beneath of four hundred tons of a highly explosive material. In an infinitesimal duration, they were evaporated across the Stygian torrent into the Elysian arena, with the subduction of the scansorial bird, who was ejaculated a league into space, over the Mississippi cataclysm, minus his pennate attachments, also an orb of sight and one pedal extremity, while his plumage was considerably incinerated. As he descended upon a timber projecting from this terrestrial sphere, on his only remaining pedal extremity, he pragmatically vocifearted, with a Machiavelian sneer:

"'Trismegistus! but that trenches on the admirable. My curiosity becomes procreated to become cognizant of what he will effectuate in the futurity!!'"

When Verbum ceased speaking, Jake Metzler (whom the reader will remember as the hero of the long retreat from Bull Run) arose and remarked: "Mr. Bresident: If I don't vas mistaken, it seems to me dot I've heard dot sthory before."

This remark was the signal for a roar of laughter, while Jake looked around in wonder at their merriment.

Verbum resumed the chair, and said: "We will now hear the report of the Chairman of the Committee on Revenge."

Joe Hart, the Chairman of the Committee, arose and began: "Mr. President: Old Jack Hall made various defamatory and threatening remarks concerning the Vandals, so the other night we greased and soaped his back porch. And the next morning, when the old codger went out to get a pail of water, his heels flew out from under him and he made an attempt to stand on his head. We also circulated a report that he whipped his wife, and it is all over the town.

"Old Morgan said we were a pack of roughs and scoundrels. And the other night we tied his clothes line across his back porch. Then we hid, and squeaked like a chicken. The old skinflint ran out to see who was stealing his hens, and tried to saw his head off on the clothes line."

"Did he succeed?" asked a Vandal.

"I think the old buccaneer did pretty well, for he's had his neck wrapped in flannel ever since."

"Mrs. Daggletail Brown says she is going to have us all arrested for slander."

"I move," said a Vandal, "that the matter be referred to the Judiciary Committee, with power to act."

It was so ordered.

"And," said the Chairman of the Judiciary Committee, "we'll give the old potwolloper all the law she wants."

"Old Molloy has lately made many threats and applied numerous epithets to us. We haven't had time to operate on the old bushwhacker yet, but expect soon to do so. Old Haskell said we were a neocracy, or words to that effect. We expect to operate on the old corsair before long."

As Hart sat down, President Verbum said: "I have been consulting with a number of the members of this body, and I would throw out as a supererogatory, metaphysical suggestion, that with this meeting the duties of the Committee on Revenge be discontinued—in other words, that its labors cease. There is an old Latin proverb which says, *Miserrima fortuna est quæ inimico caret*—That is a most miserable fortune, which is without an enemy. And undoubtedly there is a great deal of truth in the aphorism. For a person without an enemy would be a kind of nonentity—anyhow he would not be apt to have a great deal of conviviality. And the person who revenges every injury that is done him has no time for anything else. If we wish to make our lives a success, we can afford to let the dogs bark as we go by. In every community there is always a class of popinjays and old idiots who are envious of anyone whom they think is superior to them in education and intelligence, and they think it necessary to wag their slanderous tongues. The Chinese have a maxim that somewhat illustrates this point; it is: Towers are measured by their shadows, great men by those who are envious of them."

"That's *us*," said a Vandal in the rear.

"Not exactly," replied Verbum. "'Fools rush in where angels fear to tread.' But still this exemplifies the trite fact that idiots are always envious of those whom they believe to be their superiors. But the best way is to treat this class—be they tatterdemalions, walleteers or plutocrats—with silent contempt. Though, at the same time, it is well, to use the words of the philosopher Pittacus, 'To watch your opportunity.'"

As Verbum finished his discourse, Ed Thorne arose, and with a withering glance of contempt at the large dictionaries and the twelve volumes of the encyclopedia, said: "I arise for information." And with another glance of contempt at the volumes, he continued: "'Plutocrat' is neither in the dictionary or the encyclopedia. And, I suppose, 'walleteer' is not, also, but I have not searched for it. Will you be kind enough to inform me of the meaning of these words?"

"A walleteer," said Verbum, "is a second cousin to a garretcer, and first cousin to a nomad, and synonymous to a tramp. It is in the dictionary, but the other word, 'Plutocrat,' has not yet been devoured and digested by the omniverous lexicographers. A plutocrat is a person suddenly arisen from low life to wealth; a parvenu."

The motion of Stoakes, to discontinue the Committee on Revenge, was then put and carried, and Verbum then called for the report of the Chairman of the Committee on Temperance.

For the Vandal Congress had become a temperance organization. Who had been the prime mover in effecting it was an enigma none could solve. But one night, at a special meeting, they resolved themselves into a temperance body, and they did it with a great deal of style and eclat. They made speeches on temperance, and repeated and read all the Bacchanalian poetry they knew or had ever heard. Then they brought out the famous "little brown jug," full of whiskey, and put into it aquae ammoniа, aloes, asafœtida and various other nauseous mixtures, then, filling their glasses from its contents, they invited each other to drink. None of them, however, tasted the mixture except Jake Metzler, of Bull Run fame. He took a "horn," and instantly his heels flew up in the air and his head struck the floor. "Donder and blitzen!" he remarked afterward, "it liked to kilt me!"

After their carnival of fun they proceeded to business—and they did not do things by halves. They passed a set of laws making the penalty for the first offense (drinking liquor) suspension from the club for six months, and for a second, and each succeeding offense, suspension for a year. But they allowed the accused a trial before a jury of his peers, and also counsel, but at the same time they took the precaution to elect a prosecuting attorney, whose duty it was to proceed against the accused. Ed Thorne, who was a law student, had been chosen for this office.

The Chairman of the Temperance Committee arose and said: "We have but one offender to report—Jake Metzler. He was discovered *in flagrante delicto*—in the very act of drinking a glass of lager beer."

"Has any information been filed against him?" asked Verbum.

"Yes, Mr. President," replied Thorne.

"Has the accused counsel?"

"Yes," replied Pete Hale, a law student, "I am acting for the defense. And I will state that the accused pleads not guilty, and that the ground of defense is impulsive or emotional insanity." Then, turning to Bill Stoakes, a medical student, he said in a whisper: "Bill, you had better read up on 'Insanity in its Relation to Crime,' as I shall call you as an expert."

"Then," said Verbum, "the trial is set for the next regular meeting of the Congress, at which time you are expected to have your witnesses and experts here."

"Owing to the lateness of the evening," continued the President, "and the somnolence of some of the members, we will postpone the report of the Committee on Incidents of the War, and hear the report of the librarian, after which we will prorogue this session of the Congress."

Ed Thorne, the librarian, arose and said: "Since the last session we have purchased the Encyclopedia Britannica, the Imperial Dictionary, and Froissart's Chronicles, and have received by donation eight volumes."

As Thorne resumed his seat, Verbum said: "The motion to adjourn is now in order."

And in a few minutes more the lights were extinguished, and the Vandals were filing into the dark street. And now, gentle reader, wishing them godspeed and prosperity, we bid farewell to the budding potentates of the future!

CHAPTER XIX.

HOME AGAIN IN ST. ARLYLE.

> I'VE wandered on through many a clime where flowers
>   of beauty grow,
> Where all was blissful to the heart and lovely
>   to the view—
> I've seen them in their twilight pride, and in their
>   dress of morn,
> But none appeared so dear to me as the spot where
>   I was born. —*Anonymous.*

GENERAL Charles Landon, after his return from the geological expedition in South America, about four months before, had been residing in the city near St. Arlyle, but the fame he had won as a scientist had preceded him, until his renown as a scientist rivaled and even exceeded his brilliant career as a soldier. Fortune, too, that fickle goddess, had smiled generously upon him. But despite his fame and fortune, there came an almost irresistible longing to go back to the quiet little village of St. Arlyle, the home of his boyhood and early manhood, around which clung the sweetest and dearest memories of all the halcyon days of his youth, when "life seemed bathed in Hope's romantic hues." Those happy, careless days, colored in sweetest memories by the golden light of love!

Some one has said that little villages are the nearest to earthly atoms of shattered paradise, and I think that no truer words were ever written. There is a charm about a little village that a city can never possess. For in a great metropolis one's individuality is so completely buried in the large mass of people that if he falls from the ranks he is as little missed—except by his nearest circle of friends—as would be a wave on a mighty ocean's breast; but in a village there is a personality—the whole village know each other; they may gossip about one, and, to use a hyperbole, know one's own business better than he does himself. But, after all, it shows an interest in one, and often not an unkindly-feeling, though sometimes roughly expressed, but still never with that careless viciousness we too often see in a city. As we have said, the village people know nearly all about each other's affairs, and take more than a passing interest in them. The last marriage has been weighed and discussed by them, even when the young people first became engaged, and then they always throw a tinge of romance around the young couple's matrimonial bliss, with sincere wishes for their future welfare! Births, too, receive their share of attention, for when Ned and Nelly become the parents of a baby the event is thoroughly discussed. And lastly, when death reaps one of the town's citizens, there are always true regrets at his loss; for, unlike the busier world, they have time to feel and soothe another's woe.

Nearly all men keep some little village in reserve, for a home in case of mischance or misfortune, or when they become tired of the worry of society. And what a sweet rest it often proves to bankrupts in trade, mortified pleaders in courts and senates, victims of idleness and pleasure, or men who have brilliantly succeeded in the great world, but found at last that the world's greatest honors were simply dross, and what their hearts needed most was *peace and love!*

And so they are all given—regardless of their former glories, mischances or defeats—a place in the little commonwealth, and they soon learn to like the little world far better than they ever did the great one. For we nearly always find that little things are the sweetest. Little cottages are generally the most cozy, little farms the best tilled, little books the most read, little songs the most sung, little words the sweetest, little lakes the stillest, and little hearts the fullest. Everyone calls that little which he loves best and dearest on earth. And Nature, too, when she makes anything supremely beautiful and rare, makes it little—little diamonds, little pearls and little rubies. And so I shall always think that *little villages are the nearest earthly atoms of shattered paradise!*

As we have remarked, there came a longing, an irresistible desire in Landon's heart to roam again among the hills and vales of St. Arlyle. The spot around which his heart's sweetest and tenderest memories of bygone years still clung; and though he felt Bertha's love was lost to him forever, still there came a longing in his heart to revisit the old scenes, where they had spent such blissful days together, and to live them over in imagination, if not in reality. Days, as he looked back to them, that seemed embalmed with a touch of paradise. And no words can express how deeply and sincerely he regretted his rash act of doubting Bertha's constancy, and flinging away her love. "It was," he thought over and over again, "a mad, foolish course to pursue, but I have suffered dearly for it. But I deserve it all, and even more."

So one fine summer day Charles Landon left his office and turned down a street of the city leading toward the railway station, from whence the cars ran to St. Arlyle. When he reached the station, he glanced at his watch and found that he had nearly an hour to wait before the departure of the train. Nearly opposite the station stood the Academy of Art, and as he gazed toward it, he noticed an announcement in front of the building that there was then being held a grand exhibition of paintings by local and foreign artists. He was very fond of art, and quite a connoisseur of paintings, so he crossed the street and entered the Academy. There was a large crowd of spectators present, and he found the exhibition of paintings a very valuable and extensive one, so he strolled along for some time, examining them, when his attention was attracted by an unusual crowd around a painting at the farther end of the hall, which, from the attention it attracted, seemed to be the gem of the collection. As he approached it, almost at the first glance there was something that struck him as unusually familiar about the scene it represented. In a few moments he recognized the painting as a representation of the room in which he had lain wounded so many weeks after the battle of Gettysburg. That room, he felt, he could never forget, for every lineament of it was indellibly impressed on his mind, during those long days of suffering and weeks of convalescence.

The painting was simply entitled, "For His Country," and represented a medium-sized apartment, with a bed in one corner, upon which a wounded soldier was lying, while in the distance, through the open window, could be seen a battle raging, amid fire and smoke. The wounded man was attired in the full uniform of an officer, and the blood from his wounds was yet fresh, bespattering the breast of his dark blue coat, and partly crimsoning the golden star in the insignia of his rank, on one of his shoulders. His head was resting on one arm, and the face was partly turned toward the wall, but there were enough of its lineaments portrayed for Charles Landon to recognize it as a copy of his own face. The picture had evidently been painted by a master hand, and it was fascinatingly realistic to Landon, as he observed that not a particular of the scene had been omitted. The old-fashioned chairs, the stand, and the pictures on the walls, were all portrayed there, while even the red climbing roses, nodding in at the window, had not been forgotten. How well he remembered them, when, after nights of pain and delirium, he awoke and saw them on their long, pendant stems waft through the open window in the warm July air, till in his feverish imagination they seemed like human heads nodding him a good morning and endeavoring to encourage him in his struggle with death. And the mythological picture on the wall—Hercules's contest with the Nemean lion—had been reproduced with all the fidelity of the original. What memories, too, that picture awakened of those bygone days—when the spark of life flickered but feebly in his body, and his feverish brain in its semi-consciousness often took the shadow for the substance—and he gazed upon it like one under a spell, till in his feverish fancy the actors became endowed with life, and the struggle between the hero and the beast became an actual one. Then how he sympathized with the hero, and longed for his victory.

Charles Landon had become so absorbed in the contemplation of the painting, that he had grown oblivious to all around him, when he was aroused from his reverie by becoming aware that others beside himself had noticed his resemblance to the portrait. Not wishing to attract attention, he modestly turned away, but not before he had learned that the artist's name was *Bertha Merton!*

"Ah," he thought, as he saw her name in one corner of the painting, "that accounts for its fidelity to the original! Perhaps," he thought, "there may be a lingering spark of the old love in her heart. But it is hardly possible, after the brutal way I acted toward her. But still, 'there are more things in heaven and earth than are dreamed of in our philosophy.'"

Just then the last warning peals of the locomotive's bell sounded, and he hurried from the building and entered a car.

As the train approached St. Arlyle there arose before him, as if by magic, the old scenes of his boyhood he knew so well, lying clear and calm in the light of that beautiful summer afternoon. And what an association of delightful memories each hill, brook and meadow brought back to him. There at the base of the mountain, was the little lake, where he used to love to swim, while above it rose the tall mountain that he had often climbed, and while standing beneath its shady oaks, had "viewed the landscape o'er." There, too, were the blue waters of the bay, with their white-caps splashing on the sandy beach, as in the years of yore.

At last the church spires and the taller buildings of the village came full in view, lying calm and peaceful in the summer sunshine. And in his heart what a wealth of memories clung around them. There was the old haunted house on the hill, around which many a bright fancy clung, and there were the college buildings, in which he had passed many a happy day, and there, too, was the cottage on the rising ground above the river, a spot doubly dear and sweet to him, for it was Bertha's old home. At last the train ran over the bridge across the river, whose waters rippled cool and clear beneath the shadows that fringed its banks. And as the old beloved scenes broke before him, his spirits arose as if by enchantment, and he repeated almost passionately the lines of the poet:

> "I am come again with summer,
> It is lovely to behold,
> Will it welcome the newcomer,
> As it used to do of old?
> Within those dark green covers,
> Whose shade is downward cast,
> How many a memory hovers
> Whose light is from the past!"

When the train reached the station and Landon was yet stepping from the car, he was met by Colonel Tom Gleaton.

"Ah, General," said Gleaton, "Welcome back to St. Arlyle! You see the town has improved since last you saw it. It has become quite a fashionable watering-place. We publish the village paper twice a week now, and I'm its editor."

"That's the very profession that will suit your genius. In fact the one you've been looking for for years."

"No," replied Gleaton, in his facetious way, "it is journalism that has been searching for me. And I've no doubt it would have languished, had it not discovered your humble servant."

At that moment Landon was surrounded by a host of old friends, who profusely expressed their delight in welcoming him back again.

He left the station and strolled through the village, everywhere meeting with friends, who greeted him with joyous delight, for he had ever been a favorite with young and old in St. Arlyle. He visited the college an I strolled past the haunted house—no longer haunted now, but converted into a village museum and library. He stopped in front of Bertha's old home and gazed into the garden, as there arose in his heart sweet memories of those happy bygone days. Then he wandered through the tangled wood to the river, and along its bank, watching its clear, rippling waters till his heart grew buoyant and joyous, and he lived over in imagination—if not in reality —those old, enchanted days again! At last he reached the bridge, where he and Bertha first had met; and though its association aroused a host of pleasant memories, still there came just a tinge of sadness on his handsome face, as he felt she was lost to him forever, though her image would ever remain stamped on his heart. But then he thought:

" 'Tis better to have loved and lost,
Than never to have loved at all."

Man bewails, but God directs in his mysterious way. For though he dared not even dream it, he should live the old life over again, in all its fullness and all its sweetness too!

Toward the close of the afternoon, he strolled back to the bay, and, wandering along the sandy beach until he came to a ledge of granite—towering fully forty feet above the beach—he climbed to the summit of the huge rocks and stood carelessly gazing at the blue expanse of water, and over the green fields and pebbly beach. And it was a picture sufficiently beautiful to please even a taste more fastidious than his. In the distance, there gleamed the bright, thread-like waters of the river, lined on each bank by verdant willows and green, sloping meadows; while amid the evergreen foliage and climbing roses, nestled the white cottages, showing in all the glory of the summer afternoon's light; beyond lay the long stretch of mountains, covered with trees and vines, and divided by many shady ravines and nooks. At his feet ran the curving beach, covered with boulders and pebbles, that had been washed shoreward by many a winter's storm. In front lay the blue waters of the bay, reflecting the color of the azure sky above, stretching miles away, and sleeping its peaceful summer sleep, with only the low rumble of the surf to tell of the pent up fury and mighty power that lay dormant in its peaceful bosom. On the little wharf, in front of the hotel, nearly three-quarters of a mile away, were several parties of ladies and gentlemen, the gay garments of the former adding a charm to the picture, while the whole was far enough removed from the spectator to produce a pleasing and dreamy effect, viewed in the fading light of that summer afternoon. As he yet stood watching the pier, a little steamer left it, with a pleasure party on board, and bore directly toward the immense granite boulders. As the boat approached, there was the figure of a lady, with brown, curly hair, leaning on the railing of the quarter-deck, that particularly attracted his attention. Although her back was toward him there was something unusually familiar about her handsome figure.

As the little steamer was passing within thirty yards of the cliff, on which he stood, the lady suddenly turned by some unaccountable impulse and gazed in his direction. In an instant he recognized her—*it was Bertha!*

As she saw him, she seemed surprised, and laid her hand upon her bosom as if to still her fluttering heart, while the face she had schooled and controlled so often, for once played her false; for over her sweet face came a crimson blush. What a depth of mystery there is in a blush, that a word, a look, or a thought, will awaken, sending the carnation over brow and cheek, like the soft tint of a sky at sunset. Wonderful too that it is only the face, the *human face*, that can blush. It has been said that the blush of modesty tinted the first fair woman's cheek, when she first awoke in the sunny garden of Eden, and that it has lingered with Eve's fair daughters ever since. It has also been truly remarked that the face is the tablet of the soul, whereon it records its actions and its feelings. And so thought Charles Landon, as he saw her beautiful face flush, and it emboldened him, and he resolved that before another day's sunset he would win her heart, or know his fate!

In a few moments Bertha recovered her self-possession and saluted him with a graceful bow and smile. Instantly Charles Landon raised his hat in courteous recognition of her greeting, while a tender light broke over his face, and a smile played about his lips, which was plainly visible, for the steamer in passing was not more than thirty yards distant. And standing there, high among the rocks, with the waning light of that summer afternoon falling full upon his handsome face and figure, he formed a picture that an artist would have loved to paint! And no wonder, then, that a thrill of admiration crossed Bertha's face, as she noted his fine, soldierly bearing and the erect poise of his head, crowned with its dark brown, curly hair, while his handsome face was lit with a rare, sweet tenderness she remembered so well. But there came a remembrance of another time, when she had seen that face glitter with daring amid fire and smoke on the battle field of Gettysburg; but she could not help thinking that she liked it better illuminated by the light of *peace* than she did by the glitter of war.

As the little steamer glided away, the last beams of the sun were throwing a subdued glory over the dark blue water and distant hills, while amid the dying light he watched Bertha's beautiful girlish figure, on the hurricane deck, fade from view in the gathering gloom. The sun had already sunk like a great ball of refulgent fire, leaving clouds of the brightest crimson, shading into the daintiest of roses amid borders of purple and gold, with all the changing splendor of Alcinous's golden-portaled cities in his empire of the clouds!

Night had closed around, and the little figure on the hurricane deck had faded from his view as Landon turned to leave the rock, as he thought sadly: "I've little hope of winning back the old place in her heart—but still:

" 'He either fears his fate too much,
   Or his deserts are small,
Who fears to put it to the touch
   To win or lose it all!' "

CHAPTER XX.

UNDER THE LIGHT OF PEACE.

He might have took his answer long ago.—*Shakespeare.*

OH, the heart that has truly loved, never forgets,
But as truly loves on to the close,
As the sun-flower turns on her god, when he sets,
The same look which she turned when he rose.
—*Moore.*

THE next day was clear and bright, and the beautiful country around lay in the summer sunshine, as a vivid picture before him, with its dark green woods, sloping to the winding river, while the rocky hills above, at whose bases lay the green meadows, gradually slanting till they dipped into the bright blue waters of the bay, forming a fitting frame for the rose-embowered cottages of the village. And in his heart, what a world of memories clung around those familiar scenes, of the happy days gone before. So deeply had he become interested in the old scenes, lit by their sweet memories, that it was not till in the afternoon that he returned to the seaside hotel. After lunch he lit a cigar, and strolling into the park attached to the hotel, turned into a path that led through a tangle of wild roses and thick pines, toward the river. When he reached the end of the path he came to a small terrace on the bank of the river, and there, to his surprise, on a rustic bench, beneath the shadow of an oak, Bertha was sitting. He stopped suddenly, and with a wildly beating heart, leaning against a tree behind a cluster of bushes that hid him from view, while he feasted his eyes on the lovely picture she formed, as she sat thoughtfully gazing into the river.

He had always considered her pretty in the happy bygone days in St. Arlyle, but the succeeding years since then, had lavishingly ripened and perfected the girlish beauty of face and form, till now she was more than pretty—she was magnificently beautiful in all the full splendor of a woman's perfection and glory! From the small arched foot, peeping beneath her robe, to the crowning mass of curly hair that clustered around her brow—which had grown several shades darker than in former years, but which, in its contrast with her pure white face, only added to her beauty—she appeared a model that would have pleased the most fastidious artist's taste. Her face was as clear and white as marble and almost of as fine a texture; her lips were finely moulded, and, when they parted, showed perfect curves, of carmine's brightest hue; her chin was dainty and dimpled; the cheeks were finely moulded, with a shadowy dimple in each; while the straight, Grecian nose, with its delicate red nostrils, would have served for a sculptor's model. The large liquid eyes, of midnight's dreamy hue, magnificently crowned the beauty of her face, while the long, drooping lashes that fringed the white lids, only gave a deeper, darker, and more unfathomable splendor, to the velvety orbs! But yet there was a magic spell about her face that even overshadowed its loveliness—that was its rare sweetness!

But as he turned and moved toward her he noticed a sad expression on her sweet young face, that grieved him deeply. She did not notice him till he stood quite close to her; then, as she turned her head, the sad, far-away look in her soft dark eyes gave place to one of surprise.

"Ah, my lady," he said, pleasantly, "building castles in the air? Or as the French say, constructing chateaux des Espagne?"

"Oh, no," she replied, smiling, "I have been painting all morning, and came out in the open air to enjoy my *Dolce far niente.* But," she added, naively, "I'm afraid I fell into thinking, or, perhaps, dreaming of the past!"

"Why afraid?" he asked.

"Because, though pleasant moments, still they haunt, but to remind that they did not last!"

As he reached her side, she arose and held out her hand, as her heart gave a wild throb of excitement, and her face grew even paler. As he grasped her extended hand he could not help noticing how lovely her face looked in its marble-like paleness, framed by the soft brown curls. The old saucy archness was gone, but there was a sad sweetness in the large liquid eyes, and about the small mouth and dimpled cheek, that made him long to take her in his arms and caress her. He sat down beside her, and threw his hat on the bench beside her with a boyish carelessness, as she noticed that his dark hair curled in ringlets upon his white brow, just as she had loved to watch it in those bygone years. There was a tinge of sadness on his handsome face, despite his sweet boyish flow of spirits, showing that he, too, had suffered. And when he spoke, it was in an awkward, constrained manner, contrasting strangely with his usual open, frank way, and his customary brilliant and natural flow of language.

After a moment's silence, he plunged into his subject, like one would plunge into a stream, where he was not sure of his footing, or as one would do who had a matter in hand that he was eager to get through with, and seemed at a loss how to begin.

"Miss Merton," he commenced, "I wish to ask a favor of you. Will you grant it?"

"Certainly," she replied, noticing his embarrassment, and eager to help him, "if it lies in my power?"

"I love a certain young lady, and will you help me win her. I think you can aid me materially."

"Yes, if my humble efforts can assist you," she replied, dazed and bewildered, while a fearful pain seized her heart that made her struggle for breath. "Does he know?" she thought, "what he is asking? Can he imagine the pain he is inflicting? Has he no mercy. Oh, how desperately I love him. May Heaven help me to bear it!"

Then, after a desperate effort to control her feelings, she asked in a voice almost choked with tears:

"Do I know this young lady? What is her name?"

"It is *Bertha Merton!*"

Over her face there broke a light, such as a Raphael or a Murillo often dreamed of giving an angel, but never fully succeeded in leaving on canvas. A tranquil, joyous light that rendered her face grandly beautiful. He saw the sweet light of joy on her countenance, and his tongue became suddenly free and words rushed rapidly to his thoughts, as he exclaimed:

"Bertha, darling, will you forgive me? I know I don't deserve it! But still I love you dearly! You, and you only, have held the tenderest spot in my heart's affection, and it has never flagged, even for a moment, all the while we were at cross-purposes. I tried to forget you, but the more I tried, the more my heart clung to you! 'For the heart that has truly loved never forgets but as truly loves on to the close.' Will you forgive me, Bertie? And I promise you I'll never grow jealous again. Not even doubt you for a moment."

"Forgive you," she said, with a smile, as there came over her a feeling that set her nerves quivering with a strange sweet rapture. "There is nothing to forgive! And if there were I should say in the words of good Dr. Granville, 'The noblest lesson I've learned in life is to forgive, and, as far as the heart can, to forget.' But it would be an easy task for me to forgive you, if there were anything to forgive, for my heart has clung to you tenderly through all these years in spite of myself. And you know," she added, laughingly, "Leonidas, the bravest of the Greeks, was compelled to yield when the enemy gained his rear; and so with my own heart against me, and your own noble appeal what else can a poor girl do, but surrender? But," she added, with the old sauciness, "are you sure you love me truly?"

For her answer he took her in his arms and gently kissed her rosy lips for the first time in many a long day, as the little head nestled against his shoulder, while the hot blood suffused her cheeks and bosom, till they rivaled the red rose on her breast.

"So," he said, we have been playing at cross purposes all these years But as the old proverb says, 'As gold must be tried by fire, so hearts must be tried by pain,' perhaps it was Heaven's way of teaching us the lesson we ought to have learned before—the lesson of faith and trust. And let us hope that our hearts, in the crucible of pain, have been more refined and purified. But," he added teasingly, "I was not entirely without hope ever since that day you slyly kissed me, when I lay wounded on the battle field at Gettysburg, and you thought me dying."

"So you think I kissed you, when you lay so fearfully wounded!" she exclaimed, with all the old, sweet archness. "Why, what an *absurd fancy!* Why, the very idea is *preposterous!* What a conceited fellow you are! But then," she added, noticing the quizzical expression on his countenance, "you were so badly wounded that your mind wandered, and you imagined many ridiculous things. But as to kissing you, it is the most delightfully unreasonable fancy in the world! I can't even imagine how you obtained such a wild, absurd, droll and ridiculous idea! Why, your mind must have been wandering in the most visionary of dream lands!"

"I see," he said, laughingly, "you are determined to deny that kiss. But the thought of it has been sweet to me ever since; though perhaps my mind did wander."

"Of course it did! *You know it did!* What a foolish, inconsistent idea it was!"

As she finished speaking, she took up her hat, with its long white feather, and placed it jauntily on her little curly head.

"Ah," he said, banteringly, "I see you've changed the scarlet plume for a white one."

"Yes," she replied, with the old sweet archness he remembered so well, "I've had a taste of war and learned the full value of tranquility, so "I've changed the crimson plume of battle for the virgin white of peace!"

"True," he replied, smiling, "as the old Roman proverb says, *Dulce bellum inexperto*—war is sweet to him who has not tried it. And I have found it so, for my experience in four years of strife has only taught me to hate war the more, and love peace the better."

"By the way, Bertie," he continued, after a moment's silence, "what became of the blue mob cap, with gold band, you wore so long on the tented field?"

"Oh, my foraging cap, as you used to call it. I lost it, I think, at Gettysburg."

"Yes, I think you did," he said, roguishly, as he drew the cap from his pocket.

"Why," she exclaimed, "that's the identical foraging cap! The officers of your regiment presented it to me and I wore it in their honor. I know it was rather gaudy. But then," she added, with a sly glance at General Landon, "where men wore blue uniforms with crimson sashes, not to take into consideration gilt buttons and gay epaulettes—why a girl was justified in being a little bit flashy, too!"

"Why certainly she had, providing——" and he stopped.

"Providing what?" she asked, demurely.

"Providing she didn't kiss wounded soldiers."

"I tell you," she said, saucily, with a stamp of her little foot, "your mind was wandering when you imagined such an absurd thing! Why, the very idea is *perfectly preposterous!*"

They arose from the rustic bench, and arm in arm, strolled up the path along the river, beneath the shade of the trees and trailing vines. As they came in view of the bridge, across the river, Bertha said:

"They have built a new bridge, but otherwise the place is little changed. The old oak is still standing, throwing its shade, as in years gone by."

"Yes," he said, teasingly, "they have built a new one, to prevent young ladies on horseback from falling into the river."

"It may be," she said demurely, "but I don't think they need have troubled themselves about that. For most young ladies are capable of taking care of themselves—at least," she added, slyly, "I know of one."

When they reached the bridge, they walked partly across it till they reached the shade of the old oak, and then, leaning upon the railing, stood side by side, gazing into the stream for several moments in silence, watching the shining trout dart about in the clear waters of the river, when suddenly Bertha looked up and repeated archly the poet's familiar lines:

"I see the bright trout springing,
Where the wave is dark yet clear,
And a myriad flies are winging,
As if to tempt him near."

"Finish the stanza, my little lady," he said, sportively.

"I don't remember the rest," she answered, smiling.

"Then I'll repeat it for you," he said, good-humoredly:

"With the lucid waters blending,
The willow shade yet floats,
From beneath whose quiet bendings
I used to launch my boats."

They crossed the bridge and almost instinctively turned their steps toward Bertha's old home. As they walked up the hill together, on that beautiful summer afternoon, with their hearts beating wildly happy, there arose a flood of memories almost too deep for words. Memories sweet of those happy bygone days that they had passed together in the little village; days that ever seemed bathed in radiant sunshine, that each familiar spot and hill in St. Arlyle brought vividly back to their mental view; blissful years, when she took her first lessons in science and he learned his first in love! Peaceful years, but to be succeeded by those sad, thrilling years of war, out of which arose, as if by magic, the well remembered faces and forms of those who were sleeping under the sod on the battle fields of the sunny South. Sad and thrilling scenes, that touched their very hearts' core, till the walls of their memories seemed so written over—so crossed and recrossed by the events of the years that had fled, that there seemed no room for the thoughts of the present.

When they reached the brow of the hill, they met Colonel Tom Gleaton, and as he extended a hand to each, he said, in his old, impulsive way:

"Ah, the Heracleids have returned at last!"

"Yes," replied Bertha, smiling, "but it has not taken us quite three generations to do it, as it did the Greeks of old."

"True," said Gleaton, "the fates were propitious this time. And," he added, with a sly glance at each, "I think no plague will follow."

"Why," said Landon, "have you consulted the Oracle of Delphi?"

"No," he said quickly, and with an artfulness that caused the warm blood to suffuse both their faces, "I've consulted the Oracle of Cupid!"

"By the way," said Bertha, addressing Colonel Gleaton, and demurely and dexterously changing the subject, "I understand you have entered the field of journalism? How do you like it?"

"Very well indeed! It gives me a chance to perpetrate a would-be joke in print."

"They are more than would-be jokes," said Landon. "You have written some good things."

"I hope so," he replied:

"'For a little fun now and then,
Is relished by the best of men.'"

As Gleaton finished speaking, he turned around, and as they strolled along their conversation naturally turned to the missing links in the village's little commonwealth—those who had fallen in the Civil War—as Colonel Gleaton said:

"You remember poor Tom Kelly's death and burial, near the banks of the Potomac River? Well, not long since, we had his last resting place marked by a stone with the proper inscriptions cut on it. As you undoubtedly recall, he was the first of our St. Arlyle men to fall in battle."

"Yes," said General Landon, "he was a wild, erratic fellow, but he fully deserves all the tributes we can give him, for he had a warm Irish heart, and he fell bravely in the defense of his country, at duty's post."

"True," said Bertha, "he had his faults; but who has not? But, poor fellow, he was always a firm and true friend to me! And," she added warmly, "I shall ever hold a tender place in my heart for his memory!"

"Yes," said General Landon, "as we look back to the old days of the war, and recall its martyrs, Jeremiah Marshall, noble Dr. Granville, and sweet May Wilberton; his is ever among the familiar faces that arise like an apparition through the haze of history that is beginning to gather around the men and events of that troublous time!"

"True," said Bertha, "at the mention of their names, their well known faces seemed to beam upon us as they used to do in life. But let us think," she added, tenderly, "that they are all at rest in God's kingdom beyond the skies; that erratic Tom Kelly has been called from the post of duty to ranks of peace in heaven; that Jeremiah Marshall has found—after his sad and troublous life—the everlasting rest he longed so often to find; and that noble, generous Dr. Granville has found the reward he so truly deserved; and that sweet, gentle May, too, is waiting among the blest!"

"But there is one name," said General Landon, "of those old days, that of James Shackle, I'm afraid I never can recall without an anathema. For Bertha," he continued, "he came too near ruining your life and mine, for me ever to easily forgive him!"

In Bertha's large liquid eyes there came a sweet forgiving tenderness, as she said: "Let us not condemn him too harshly, for perhaps the great troubles and trials he had passed through had overbalanced his mind, and he was not really accountable for his later actions. Anyhow, she added, "we in our great happiness can easily afford to forgive him!"

"Ah Bertha," said Charles, smiling, "spoken like your own true, noble self—ever forgiving and forgetting!"

When they reached the garden gate of Bertha's old home, the star-spangled banner was floating from the tall flag-pole in front of it; for it was the Nation's birthday. And as they watched the gentle breeze waft out in the balmy sunlight, the gay folds of the bonny red, white and blue, Bertha said:

"The old flag floats as proudly as if it had never been riddled by shot and shell in internal strife."

"Yes," said Gleaton, in his facetious way, "I never see the old flag, but it reminds me of bullets and balls coming in my direction."

"Or," said Bertha, mischievously, "riding off the battlefield on a cannon."

"Perhaps," he said, smiling good-humoredly, though the joke was at his expense, "but I hope," he added, "those days are over forever."

"God grant that they are," said Charles Landon, earnestly, "and that unlike the nations that have gone before, suicide may never be the fate of the American Republic!"

And kind reader, let us too hope, that if war comes in this passing generation, it will find the Blue and the Gray in the same line of battle, fighting side by side, a common foe!

As Landon finished speaking, Gleaton turned down the hill, while Charles and Bertha entered the gate hand in hand, and in the waning light of that glorious summer afternoon, strolled along a familiar rose-bordered path, and there, gentle reader—whilst his arm is encircling her dainty waist, and her dark golden head is nestling on his shoulder—we leave them, under the sway of the greatest magic wand of all—*the transforming light of love!*

So their hearts, like their country's flag, had passed through *War to Peace!*

THE END.

www.ingramcontent.com/pod-product-compliance
Lightning Source LLC
Chambersburg PA
CBHW031400160426
43196CB00007B/835